RICH!
TEEN FINANCIAL PLANNING

Karin Humbolt

The Reynolds Publishing Company, LLC

Overland Park, Kansas

Rich! Teen Financial Planning

Written by Karin Humbolt

Library of Congress Control Number 2026904633

ISBN 978-0-9665128-3-0

Published and manufactured in the United States of America

Direct inquiries to:

The Reynolds Publishing Company, LLC
9727 Antioch Road, #13535
Overland Park, KS 66212

DEDICATION

Rich! Teen Financial Planning is dedicated to my father, a hard-working, kind, and loving man who showed me the way.

My financial planning books, including *Rich! Teen Financial Planning,* were originally inspired by a money management seminar I taught to a teacher-client's 10th-grade class. On the day of the seminar, I was besieged with questions from the students. I learned a valuable lesson that day. Teenagers have as much curiosity, questions, and misconceptions about money and investments as adults.

In 1998, my first financial planning book for teens entitled, *I Want To Be Rich! A Teenager's Modem To Money,* was published.

In 2017, *I Want To Be Rich! Financial Planning for Teens* was published. In 2007 and 2017 the Spanish translations entitled *¡Quiero Ser Rico! Planificación Financiera Para Jóvenes* were published.

Rich! Teen Financial Planning is not a story of how to be a billionaire or the richest person on the planet. It is a philosophy of how to live your life. Not only is this book dedicated to my father, it is dedicated to the teenagers of the world. To achieve a solid financial future, be persistent. Never give up! Be kind to others!

ACKNOWLEDGEMENTS

To all my friends, clients, and followers who have shared their dreams and allowed me to be a part of those dreams. Be strong, positive, and patient, and show kindness and love to those around you. May you be rich in health, wealth, and wisdom!

CONTENTS

CHAPTER 1
INTRODUCTION
Balance Your Life & Your Money

Want to buy something and you don't think you can afford it? If the answer is yes, then *Rich! Teen Financial Planning* is the book for you.

Do you like money? Do you hear social media influencers, teachers, journalists, or friends speak about the stock market and wonder what they're talking about? Does the name **Dow Jones Industrial Average** make as much sense as a foreign language you do not speak? If your answer is "Yes," this is the book for you.

Do you want to go to college but don't think you can afford it? Do you want a job that pays more than minimum wage? Do you have enough money?

These are a few of the subjects covered in this book: spending, saving, and investing–also known as money management.

Throughout my career as a commercial real estate broker and as a **financial advisor**, I have helped adults achieve financial freedom.

Many of my clients were educators, including university professors and high school teachers. As a real estate professional, I help clients and customers grow their real estate holdings. My clients are no different than you when it comes to knowledge or lack of knowledge about the management of money and investments.

Years ago, when I was very young, I inherited some money. The result? I spent it very quickly. If I had invested the money, that $20,000 would be worth approximately $86,450 today if it averaged a 5% annual *return*; $349,000 if it averaged a 10% annual return; and $1,324,500 if it averaged a 15% annual return!

At the time, spending seemed like a good idea. However, money is far easier to spend than it is to earn. I started my real estate career and became a financial advisor so I'd never make that mistake again!

My interest in writing this book was spurred by a request from a teacher to conduct a money management seminar for her tenth-grade class. After my presentation, I was besieged with questions from teens like yourself. The questions ranged from how to balance a checkbook to what a mutual fund is.

I learned a valuable lesson that day. Teenagers have as much curiosity, questions, and misconceptions about money and investments as adults!

If I could show you how to make $1,000,000, would you be interested? However, with the price of goods and services rising (a common occurrence known as **inflation**) a million dollars might not be enough. Is that difficult to believe? The point of this book is to help you understand money management and the making of money from money in simple language.

Please keep in mind, this book is a basic money management primer for teens. This is only a beginning to what you should spend a lifetime exploring. Money, how to make it, invest it, and keep it.

My intention is to give you suggestions to take the mystery out of money management. In this book you will find do's and don'ts about investments and how to develop good saving and spending habits. By following these tips you will learn how to accumulate more money in the long run than your parents and grandparents.

This book shows you how to balance your life and your money. For instance, there is a theory, referred to as **yin and yang**, that says for every action there is an opposite reaction. Yin and yang represent the need for balance. When it comes to money management, you will need balance.

You should know that the best secret to accumulating money and wealth is time! As a teen, time is on your side. While the secret of time alone will not make you a millionaire, if you practice this book's tips and suggestions, you will know more about money and the making of money than most adults.

Throughout this book, you will find words that are italicized and highlighted in bold type. The definitions of these words are found in this book's *Glossary* at the back of the book. Also, if you come across a word you don't understand, check the definition in a dictionary. This practice of studying the definitions of unfamiliar words will help you to better understand the subject matter.

I recommend that you keep a notebook, paper, pens, and pencils nearby while reading this book. Some chapters include practice exercises that will require writing materials.

The Information Resources section included at the back of this book will further increase your knowledge of money management. Make use of these sources of information in order to balance your life and your money.

How do we get started toward the accumulation of money?

Read on to *Chapter 2 – Setting Goals*, to learn how to balance your life

and your money.

CHAPTER 2
SETTING GOALS
Your First Step To Financial Freedom

Setting and *implementing* goals is first and foremost in your pursuit of accumulating money.

Webster's New World Dictionary defines the word goal as: "1. the line or place at which a race, trip, etc. is ended; 2. an object or end that one strives to attain; aim."

Why set goals? Because you need a beginning and a destination. If you don't know what you are aiming for or where you are going, the chance of achieving anything substantial is slim to none.

Imagine taking a vacation to a place you've never been before. If you don't know your destination or don't have a road map or GPS (Global Positioning System), your journey will be difficult.

Setting goals is the perfect way to start your journey toward financial success. Your goals will be your road map to financial freedom!

Here are some questions to ask yourself before setting goals:

1.   **What financial goals do I want to achieve?** Do I want to buy a cell phone, new clothes, a computer, a car, pay for college, live on my own, go on vacation, buy a house, save for retirement?

2.   **When do I want to achieve my financial goals?** Next week, next month, in a year, five years? The more time you have, the easier it is to achieve your goals.

3.   **How will I achieve my goals?** The answer to this question will be the nuts and bolts that make your goals and dreams come true.

Set both short-term and long-term goals. For many adults, short-term goals may include time periods of one to five years. As a teenager, your time frame for short-term goals may be considerably shorter, say one to six months and up to one year.

Long-term goals for adults are five years and longer, say ten, twenty, or even thirty years. That's probably unrealistic for you at this stage. For purposes of discussion, let's consider your long-term goals to be one to five years. Now let's get started.

The first rule for setting goals is:

- **Write your goals down. In a notebook, on your phone, or on a tablet. Repeat after me. Write down your goals!**

Let's start with a short-term goal exercise. Sit at a table with this book, pens, and your notebook. **Ask yourself the following questions:**

- **What do I want to buy?**

- **How much will it cost?**

- **When do I want, or need it?** Be realistic.

- **How will I earn the money?**

As you answer each question, number and write down your answers. For example:

1. **What do I want to buy?** A cell phone.

2. **How much will it cost?** $1,000.

3. **When do I want it?** Within 3 months.

You want to purchase a cell phone that costs $1,000 in three months. Three months equals twelve weeks. Divide $1,000 by twelve weeks. $1,000 / 12 weeks = $83.33 per week. **Therefore, you will**

need to save $83.33 each week to purchase the item.

4. **How will I earn the money?** Allowance. Chores for parents, adult relatives, neighbors, or adult friends of parents. A part-time job or small business.

Now let's cover long-term goals:

1. **What do I want to buy?** A car.

2. **How much will it cost?** $10,000.

3. **When do I want, or need it?** (Next week, but Mom and Dad won't let you drive until you're sixteen.) Three years.

You want to purchase a car that costs $10,000 in three years. We're talking used car. What is realistic is obtainable. $10,000 divided by 3 years equals $3,333 per year. $3,333 divided by 52 weeks per year equals $64.10 per week.

$$\$10,000 \ / \ 3 \text{ years} = \$3,333 \text{ per year}$$

$$\$3,333 \ / \ 52 \text{ weeks} = \$64.10 \text{ per week}$$

Does $64.10 per week seem more obtainable than $10,000? Of course, other costs such as insurance and licenses must be considered. Not to worry, we'll cover that in *Chapter 4 – Making A Budget.*

4.   How will I earn the money?   The answer to this question is similar to the answer for short-term goals. Allowance. Chores for parents, adult relatives, neighbors, or adult friends of parents. Part-time job, small business, or full-time summer job.

When deciding "How will I earn the money?" for short or long-term goals, be creative. For example, many parts of the United States experience snow days. Next time you're missing a day at school due to snow, why not play the part of ***entrepreneur?*** Instead of social media or watching television, make money shoveling snow from driveways and sidewalks. You may be surprised by the number of jobs you acquire from adults who are either elderly, out of shape, or too busy to shovel the snow themselves.

In addition, many adults are working small businesses from home. A small business requires the typing and filing of documents. And clerical work is an easier job than shoveling snow!

Note: Interested in being an entrepreneur and owning your own business? We'll cover this subject in *Chapter 15 – You're The Boss.*

For each of your goals, complete the above exercise. Make two separate lists. One for short-term goals and the second for long-term goals. Don't set too many goals at once. Start with one or two goals in each category.

The second rule of setting goals is:

- **Review your goals often. In other words, don't write your goals in a notebook and misplace it.**

Reviewing your goals once a day is a good habit to establish. Take ten minutes and read your goals and how you will achieve those goals out loud. Yes! Say your goals out loud. Look into a mirror as you recite your goals. This is a good reinforcement of your goals.

In Napoleon Hill's book, *Think and Grow Rich*, the importance of repeating goals to yourself daily is discussed. Through repetition your goals will register not only in your conscious mind, but also in your subconscious mind. In other words, when you live, breathe, and feel your goals, you will also begin to achieve your goals.

The third rule of setting goals is:

- **Revise your goals only as needed.**

Choose your goals with plenty of thought and stick to them. However, changing situations may require changing your goals from time to time. I don't recommend changing your goals often or without plenty of thought. If you do need to revise some of your financial goals, return to the goal setting exercise and repeat the steps.

In review, to determine and achieve your goals:

- **Write your goals in a notebook, on your phone, or on a tablet.**

- **Review your goals often.**

- **Revise your goals only as needed.**

One of the first financial goals you should set for yourself is a regular savings plan. Read on to *Chapter 3 – Saving & Investing.* You are on your way to financial freedom!

CHAPTER 3
SAVING & INVESTING
Time Is On Your Side

Now that we've discussed the importance of setting goals, it's important to make saving and investing one of your goals. Systematic saving and investing is the practice of saving and/or investing money on a regular basis. This can be weekly or monthly.

If you learn one thing from this book, plan to establish and stick with a regular saving and investing plan.

Why save on a regular basis, you ask? The reason is this. If you don't save first, before spending your money, you may never start saving … or at least not until you are an older adult.

As a teenager, time is on your side. That statement is correct because a secret to accumulating wealth and money is to start early!

For instance, suppose you invested $2,000 at 17 years of age in a traditional *individual retirement account (IRA)* and never invested again. You also did not touch that investment until you retire at 55 years of age, or 38 years later.

Depending upon the source, the historical rate of return for the major stock indexes from the 1920s to today have averaged from 10% to 12% a year, or higher.

Let's be conservative and assume your investment had a 10% average annual rate of return. After 38 years your $2,000 investment at an annual return of 10% could grow to approximately $78,500. If the annual return was 12%, your $2,000 investment could grow to approximately $148,500. That's what is meant by time being on your side!

To start your saving and investing plan, select a fixed percentage of your allowance or salary as your savings goal. Before you spend a dime of that allowance or salary, put your savings into a bank savings account. Saving first translates into "pay yourself first."

The theory of "pay yourself first" works on the principle of, "if you don't pay yourself first, nobody's going to do it for you." This is true for teenagers as well as adults.

When deciding an amount to save on a regular basis, be realistic. Attempting to save 20% of your allowance each month does not make sense if you're always withdrawing from the savings account because you're running short of spending cash.

Americans are notoriously skimpy savers. A recent *Bankrate* report surveyed more than 1,000 U.S. adults about their ability to handle a surprise bill. The study found that 59% of Americans don't have enough savings to cover an unexpected $1,000 emergency expense.

Be realistic when deciding what amount of your income you will save. Save as much as possible, but most importantly, start saving something on a regular basis.

Why save or invest? Making money from money is the only way most people can earn money without physically working for it.

There are numerous ways to make money from money. At this stage, you're probably most familiar with saving money in a savings account at a local bank. Most banks in the United States are federally insured, which means you are guaranteed by the full faith and credit of the United States government to receive back whatever you put into your savings account plus interest.

The drawback to saving in a bank savings account is the interest paid by banks is low compared to other types of investment earnings. Interest on bank savings accounts can range from 1% to 3% or more. Interest this low won't make anyone wealthy.

However, keeping a bank savings account for short-term savings goals and emergencies is a good idea. In fact, it's convenient because your money is easily accessible, it's guaranteed, and typically you won't pay a penalty for withdrawing your money.

Another method of saving is investing in U.S. savings bonds. When the bond is cashed at ***maturity***, you will be paid the ***face amount*** of the bond. The face amount equals the amount paid for the bond plus interest.

Some people like to save by investing in real estate. A drawback to real estate investment is the large amount of ***down payment*** that is often needed to get started. If you borrow money from a bank to buy a house, most lending institutions will require as much as 20% for a down payment. We'll discuss more about real estate in *Chapter 11 – Real Estate: The American Dream.*

Some people turn to stamp or coin collections, baseball cards, antiques, or gold and silver ***bullion*** as investments. These types of investments can be risky and are only recommended for investors willing to thoroughly research the investment.

As you may be aware, millions of Americans and people all over the world invest in the stock market. A person who invests in the stock market basically owns a piece of the company by purchasing shares of stock. We'll discuss the stock market in *Chapter 8 – Stocks: The Place To Be.*

Other people choose to own a piece of hundreds of different companies by investing in **mutual funds**. We'll discuss mutual funds in *Chapter 9 – Mutual Funds: Convenient Investing.*

Individuals who prefer investments that pay a steady income may choose government or corporate **bonds**. The subject of bonds will be covered in *Chapter 7 – Bonds: The Conservative Investment.*

Whatever method of investment you choose, it's important to learn as much as possible about that type of investment. Become as informed as possible about your investments.

At this stage, it is best to open your own savings account at a bank, savings and loan association, or credit union. Shop around by visiting several different banks. Ask what rate of interest each bank pays and any other features available to you by opening a savings account. Comparison shopping is good because the amount of interest paid may vary at each savings institution.

Having your own savings account, as well as a checking account, builds good **credit**. Having good credit will help you obtain loans for cars, college, an apartment, or a home in the future. We'll discuss this subject in more detail in *Chapter 16 – Credit & Credit Cards: A Word of Caution.*

As mentioned previously, choose a percentage of your allowance or income from your job as your savings goal. Or you may want to choose a certain dollar amount. **At first, it is not important how much you save, just get into the habit of saving!**

Your savings goal can be for short-term financial goals, long-term financial goals, and for emergency money. Whatever the purpose, saving is a very important habit that should stay with you all your life. The sooner you start your savings habit, the better!

Remember to:

- **Pay yourself first!**

- **Select a realistic amount to save on a regular basis.**

- **Stick with your savings program.**

For tips on how much you should save and spend, read on to

Chapter 4 – Making A Budget: It's Not A Puzzle!

CHAPTER 4
MAKING A BUDGET
It's Not A Puzzle

Have you ever taken a trip to a place you've never visited? Would you search and struggle to find your way like someone in the dark without a light? It would make more sense to follow a roadmap to reach your destination. Such is the case with a financial plan. To reach your financial goals, it's important to have a financial roadmap, otherwise known as a budget.

In this chapter, we will develop three monthly budgets. First, we will design a budget to fit your present circumstances, known as **"Your Budget Now."** Second, we will make adjustments to help you learn how to live within a budget, known as **"Your Adjusted Budget."** Third, we will design a future budget for when you go to college or live on your own. This budget is known as **"On Your Own Budget."**

Let's get started with your personalized budget. Complete the following exercise to track your spending habits.

1.   **Each day, record every purchase and the amount spent in your notebook.**

2. **Continue this exercise for one month.**

3. **At the end of the month total your expenses.** By tracking your expenses, you will get an accurate record of how much you are spending each month.

Keeping track of your expenses in writing is an eye-opening experience. The results may astonish you. This exercise will reveal why you are often short of money, even if you have a job. When you discover what you are buying and how much it costs, you are ready to design a budget for your present circumstances. It's called "Your Budget Now."

On a sheet of paper, make a column on the left-hand side labeled "Income." Underneath and several lines down label the next column "Expenses."

Under the "Income" column write the source and amount of money you earn monthly. Monthly income includes your allowance, money from part-time and full-time jobs, gifts from relatives, etc. When designing any budget, money from jobs will be ***net income***.

That is your income after all taxes have been deducted.

Under the "Expenses" column list your expenses and the monthly dollar amounts. Expenses include:

1. **Savings.** Determine the amount of money, percentage of income, or dollar amount you will save each month. Label this item "Savings" and enter the dollar amount. It does not matter if the amount is only $1.00 per month. The lesson is to get in the habit of saving on a regular basis. Therefore, you will learn to save for those upcoming concert tickets, clothes, a car, college funds, or whatever you need to save for in the future.

2. **Tithing.** This is the practice of contributing a percentage of your income to the religious organization of your choice.

3. **Personal items.** Shampoo, make-up, haircuts, and clothing.

4. **Entertainment costs.** Movies, concerts, and sporting events.

5. **Food.** Meals away from home, snacks, lunches, and dinners out.

6. **Transportation costs.** Mass transit, transportation fares

such as taxis, ride-sharing, and car expenses such as gasoline, oil changes, maintenance, repairs, car payments, insurance, and registration and licensing fees.

7. **Miscellaneous expenses.** Any other expenses.

Now total all expenses at the bottom of the budget worksheet. If you have some quarterly, semiannual, or annual expenses, divide the amount by the appropriate number of months to arrive at a monthly dollar amount. For example: If car insurance costs $600 semiannually, divide the $600 by 6 months to arrive at a cost of $100 per month for automobile insurance.

In the following "Your Budget Now" example, the teen has something in common with many Americans today. This individual spends more money than they earn, as you can see by the ***net loss*** of $159.00 per month.

YOUR BUDGET NOW

INCOME

Allowance	$ 40.00
Part-time job (net)	$200.00
Total Income	**$240.00**

EXPENSES

Savings (10%)	$ 24.00
Personal	$ 60.00
Entertainment	$ 80.00
Food	$ 75.00
Transportation	$160.00
Total Expenses	**($399.00)**
Net Gain	**$0**
Net Loss [$240 - $399] =	**($159.00) per month**

At the bottom of your budget, subtract your total expenses from your total income. If your expenses are more than your income, you will need to make adjustments. Here are some suggestions:

- **Sacrifice some of your entertainment by going out less or by finding less expensive alternatives.** This may be a painful option, but for some teenagers it is the only category where expenses can be lowered.

- **Work more hours, or find a better paying job.**

- **Negotiate a larger allowance by taking on additional responsibilities at home.**

- **Eat out less.** Cooking at home is healthier and less expensive than eating out.

- **If you drive a car, watch your gasoline consumption.** Cruising eats dollars $$$.

The following "Your Adjusted Budget" provides tips for an income that exceeds expenses. For instance, our teenager **negotiates** with parents to receive a larger allowance in exchange for tackling more jobs at home. The larger allowance accounts for $40.00

additional income per month.

Entertainment expenses were originally high compared to the amount of income. By streaming or renting movies instead of going to theaters and by watching sporting events on mobile devices instead of in person, our teenager saves $40 a month.

Food expenses were also high. By eating more at home, our teenager cut this expense by $45.00 per month.

Cost cutting also took place with transportation. With less cruising, transportation costs were cut by $60.00 per month. Or the teen could use mass transit.

Since savings is based on 10% of income, the monthly savings has now increased to $28.00 per month. Due to the increase of income and decrease in expenses, our teenager now has a ***net gain*** of $22.00 instead of a net loss!

YOUR ADJUSTED BUDGET

INCOME

Allowance $ 80.00

Part-time job (net) $200.00

Total Income   **$280.00**

EXPENSES

Savings (10%) $ 28.00

Personal $ 60.00

Entertainment $ 40.00

Food $ 30.00

Transportation $100.00

Total Expenses   **$258.00**

Net Gain   [$280 - $258] =**   **$ 22.00 per month

Net Loss   **$ 0**

You can brainstorm and think of some income increasing and expense cutting ideas. Under no circumstances do I suggest sacrificing homework or fun time. Instead work your budget smarter!

Once you've created a budget for your present circumstance, start work on a future budget. The purpose of "On Your Own Budget" is to learn how a budget works if you live on your own or attend a postsecondary school. This budget exercise will give you a new perspective on what goods and services actually cost. Far too often where money is concerned it's, "Easy come, easy go."

This budget begins the same way as did "Your Budget Now." On a new sheet of notebook paper, list "Expenses" on the left and the monthly dollar amount to the right (see "On Your Own Budget" on a following page).

You may not be familiar with the costs of living on your own. Therefore, research the cost of these expenses. Most of this research can be done online or by calling and asking questions. For purposes of explanation, I'll supply some dollar amounts. However, to benefit the most from this exercise, do your own research.

The following are suggestions for developing "On Your Own Budget":

1.   **Allocate a set percentage of your income for savings.** Since *hypothetically* you are living on your own for the first time, you'll probably need most of your money to survive. Therefore, let's use 3% of income for savings with that equaling $60.00 per month.

2.   **If you're living on your own, you'll need a place to live.** How much would rent cost for an apartment? If you don't know, contact several apartment complexes and ask what the monthly rent for a small apartment would cost.

3.   **While you're speaking with the apartment manager, ask what utilities are included in the rent.** Utilities could include electricity, natural gas, water, sewer, trash, internet, and cable service. If you, as the *tenant*, must pay some or all utilities, ask the manager what the cost of utilities averages per month. Or call the local utility company and ask what utilities average per month for an apartment in that area.

4.   **The cost of food.** Write down everything you eat in a week, at home or out. Check the cost of the food at the grocery

store, total it for the week, and multiply by four weeks to get the monthly cost of food at home. You should include the basics like vegetables, fruits, bread, milk, nuts, and meat. Next add the cost of food you eat out such as fast foods and home delivered pizza.

5.   Transportation costs. This category will be moderate to very expensive depending upon the type of transportation you choose. If you choose public transportation this expense may be relatively inexpensive.

a.   Do you want a *new* car? The car payment for a $30,000 car could be over $500 per month. For our example, we used a $350 per month car payment for a used car.

b.   Next, you'll need car insurance so you can legally drive this vehicle. The more expensive the car, the more expensive the insurance! You've probably heard insurance for teenagers is expensive. It is. For our example, we'll use $150 per month. Ask insurance agents what auto insurance for a teenager your age would cost for the car you want to purchase.

c.   If you're going to the trouble of buying this car and

paying for the insurance, you're going to need gasoline. A car also requires upkeep that includes regular oil changes and maintenance.

6. **Clothing.** If you live in a moderate climate, clothing expense could be less than for people living in northern states that require both winter and summer clothing. Look at the price tags where you shop. Estimate what was paid in a year for your clothes and divide by 12 months.

7. **Personal items.** Shampoo, soap, toothpaste, deodorant, make-up, razors, mouthwash, etc. Price these items at grocery, pharmacy, retail and discount stores.

8. **Entertainment.** Concert tickets, sporting events, movie tickets and rentals, golf fees, trips and vacations.

Once you learn what your expenses will include and how much they will cost, add them together. This will give you a realistic picture of what it costs to live on your own and how much income you will need to earn.

ON YOUR OWN BUDGET

Monthly Expenses

Savings and Investments (3%)	$ 60.00
Rent	$ 750.00
Utilities (electricity, natural gas, internet and cable)	$ 95.00
Food	$ 160.00
Transportation (car payment, insurance, gasoline & maintenance)	$ 585.00
Clothing	$ 65.00
Personal	$ 40.00
Entertainment	$ 45.00
Total Expenses	**$1,800.00**

Remember, these expenses are basic. We'll assume:

- You have furniture to furnish the apartment, dishes, tableware, pots, pans and skillets.

- You've already paid the apartment security deposit.

- You don't have a bunch of speeding tickets that hike your insurance rates sky high.

- Your parents pay for your medical insurance.

- You don't go through two tanks of gasoline a week cruising the streets.

- Your apartment doesn't catch fire and you lose everything because you didn't have renter's insurance.

- You don't go to movies, concerts, and eat expensive dinners out every night. Everyone needs to have some fun, however, entertainment expenses can bankrupt a budget.

Considering our relatively modest budget, we've already reached $1,800 per month for expenses! Remember, this is money you must **net**. Just because your job pays $1,800 per month doesn't mean you'll be able to meet your expenses. In fact, you would not be able

Rich!

to pay all your bills because federal, state, Social Security, and local taxes must be paid. These taxes can lessen your take-home pay by 15% to 25%, or higher! In other words, if you were earning $1,800 per month, taxes could reduce that amount to less than $1,530 per month. To pay $1,800 in bills per month you'll need to earn approximately $2,120 per month.

Gross Income **Needed**	**$2,120**
Less Taxes (15%)	**($ 318)**
Net Income Needed	**$1,802**

The "On Your Own Budget" could need more financial adjustments than your present budget. In the long run, you'll have to decide what expenses you can afford and what expenses you should do away with. The decision is yours.

Tips for reducing expenses include:

1.   **Lower your rent expense by choosing a less expensive place to live or having a roommate to split rent costs.**

2.   **Utilities.** Turn off the televisions, stereos, lights and any

other electronic devices when you're not using them. Turn off or adjust heating and air conditioning thermostat when you leave.

3. **Reduce the number of meals you eat away from home.**

4. **If your transportation costs are high, use public transportation, Uber or Lyft, or buy a used car for lower payments and less insurance costs, instead of an expensive new car.** However, when buying a used car, you will need to carefully shop. You don't want to acquire a "lemon" that will cost more to maintain and repair than a newer car that is covered by a warranty. Before making a deal, have a used car inspected by an automobile mechanic recommended by friends or relatives.

5. **Compare clothing prices at different stores.** You'll want to buy sturdy, well-made clothing for the lowest prices.

6. **Entertainment expenses can be expensive … they can make or break your budget.** When you first go out on your own, you'll need every dollar. Many clubs and churches offer discount group rates for entertainment events. Social organizations offer group events that involve inexpensive activities such as biking, hiking, camping, etc. Some museum visits are low cost or free. Keep your

entertainment costs to a minimum. Be creative in your pursuit of entertainment, and you'll find inexpensive alternatives.

Costs for tuition and books for vocational schools, colleges, or universities were not included in our budget. In *Chapter 13 – Higher Education: Your Key To The Future*, we'll discuss financing your education.

Is it difficult to believe that it takes this much money to afford only basic expenses? Supporting yourself is a tremendous financial responsibility.

When you turn eighteen, perhaps breaking out on your own should be postponed for several years in order to obtain a higher education. A higher education that could ensure a well-paying profession would be a wise choice. As this edition is being written, Artificial Intelligence, known as AI, is consuming a lot of media and financial attention. Do good research and choose a profession that will grow into the future. A good education will enable you to earn the type of money as an adult that will support the lifestyle to which you want to become accustomed!

In review:

- **Track your expenses.**

- **Design a budget that includes income and expenses.**

- **Eliminate unnecessary expenses.**

- **Be creative to increase your income.**

As we've seen, to establish a budget, it's important to know how much you make and spend. An important part of tracking how much you spend is to keep your checking account balanced. In *Chapter 5 – Your Checking Account: Without The Mystery*, we'll discuss this strategy.

CHAPTER 5
YOUR CHECKING ACCOUNT
Without The Mystery

A convenient way to spend money and establish credit is to have a checking account at a bank, credit union, or savings and loan association. If you prefer to use a credit card, be sure to read *Chapter 16 – Credit & Credit Cards: A Word of Caution.*

Before moving on to the topic of checking accounts, know that sometimes using cash can help curtail your spending rather than using a checking account or a credit card.

Here are some important checking account tips:

1.   **There are two parts to a checking account.** The checks you write and the **checkbook register** you maintain. The register is a record of every check you write and deposit you make. By keeping your checkbook *reconciled* (known as balanced), you'll know how much money you have in your account.

2.   **Write the amount of the check in your checkbook**

register.

3. **Write the amount of the deposit in your checkbook register.** The idea is to have more money deposited than withdrawn.

4. **When you receive your monthly statement from your bank, don't throw the statement away or put it in a drawer never to be found again.** If you bank online, print out the monthly statement. Put the statement in a file folder, specifically for your checking account, and as soon as possible, reconcile your checkbook.

To reconcile your checkbook, it means that total deposits and total checks written on the bank statement match the balance in your checkbook. If you reconcile your bank statement when you receive it, the task will be simple.

There are few things more unpleasant than trying to reconcile a checkbook that has been neglected for three to six months. It's frustrating, time-consuming, and simply much easier to reconcile your checkbook every month.

Directions on your bank statement will explain how to reconcile your checkbook with the statement. However, briefly, here's how to reconcile your checking account:

1.   List and total all checks and other debits in your checkbook register that are not listed on your statement (also include any service charges).

2.   List and total all deposits and other credits in your checkbook register that are not listed on your statement (also include interest, if any).

3.   To the *ending balance* listed on your statement, add the total credits listed in #2, and then subtract total debits listed in #1.

4.   The dollar amount you reach by adding credits and subtracting debits should be the same amount as your checkbook balance.

Again, the big secret to keeping your checkbook up to date and accurate, so you know how much you have in your checking account, is to make a habit of reconciling your checking account as soon as possible each month. If you let months go by, what would normally have taken a few minutes may take hours!

In addition, banks offer online banking. Using a computer and mobile devices, you can access your bank account information 24 hours a day, seven days a week.

Remember to:

- **Record all checks written in your checkbook register.**

- **Record all deposits in your checkbook register.**

- **Reconcile your checkbook monthly.**

Now that we've discussed how to keep track of your money, let's go on to *Chapter 6 – Taxes & Inflation*, two items that can really take a bite out of your earnings and investments.

CHAPTER 6
TAXES & INFLATION
Hidden Costs

Taxes and **_inflation_** are two subjects that many adults do not understand. Your investment strategy must take taxes and inflation into consideration. Why? Because taxes and inflation can take a big bite out of the money you earn and the profit you make on your investments!

Taxes are the money collected to pay local, state, and federal **_expenditures_** such as roads, schools, highways, freeways, sidewalks, public sewer and water systems. Everyone who earns a salary, owns a business, or makes money on investments pays taxes. Depending upon where you live, the cost of local and state taxes will vary. Also, how much you pay in taxes is determined by your **_tax bracket_**.

Federal, state, and local taxes take a large bite out of many Americans' paychecks. Simply because you earn $25.00 per hour does not mean your paycheck will equal $25.00 times the number of hours worked. Your paycheck will equal the per hour amount times hours worked, less federal, state, local, and **Social Security taxes**. What remains after taxes are paid is your **disposable income** or net income.

Your gross income - taxes = net income

Money earned on investments is also taxable since it is considered **unearned income**. You will want a sizable portion of your investments to earn a return that will pay taxes and still make a reasonable profit for you. There are a few investments that are not entirely taxed or are **tax-deferred**. The tax on a traditional individual retirement account (IRA) is not paid until the money is withdrawn at retirement. Taxes are also deferred on the interest (income) paid on **annuities** until money is withdrawn at retirement.

Then there is inflation. Inflation is a factor that should be seriously taken into consideration. **Inflation is the rate of increase, expressed as a percentage, that goods and services increase (or decrease, known as deflation) per year.**

If each year it costs more money to live, it doesn't take long for goods and services to get expensive. Historically, inflation has averaged approximately 3% per year in the United States. For example, at 3% inflation, a yearly college tuition cost of $5,000 would increase over five years to approximately $5,800 per year! That's a total increase of approximately 16% **compounded.**

In recent years, college-cost inflation has ranged from 5% to 8% per year. At 6% inflation for five years, that $5,000 yearly tuition increases to approximately $6,700 per year; an increase of approximately 34% compounded!

There is no doubt that inflation can take a financial toll. In *Chapter 13 – Higher Education: Your Key to the Future*, we will discuss how to overcome the expensive costs of additional schooling.

In review:

- **The salary you earn is reduced by federal, state, local, and Social Security taxes.**

- **The income earned from investments is taxed.**

- **When planning future expenses, consider what that product or service may cost in the future due to inflation.**

Now it is time to explore specific types of investments. In

Chapter 7, we will first consider bonds.

CHAPTER 7

BONDS

The Conservative Investment

Many investors consider **bonds** a safe and conservative type of investment. Bonds often are the financial backbone of a city, county, state, or even the federal government because they pay for the cost of roads, highways, airports, schools, and city renovation. Corporations also issue bonds to finance large *capital* (large-cap) improvements.

In the world of investments, securities are either debt or *equity instruments*. A *bond* is a *debt instrument* and represents a superior promise to repay the bondholder's investment.

A superior promise to pay means a bond investor will be paid their investment back before *common stock shareholders* if the company files for *bankruptcy*. Therefore, bonds usually are considered a more conservative or safer approach to investing than owning common stock, which is an equity investment. However, if a government entity (federal, state, or local government) or corporation is financially in trouble, then its bonds may be poorly rated and considered high-risk. Some bonds are riskier than the common stock of good companies.

Bonds may be purchased in two different ways:

- A bond may be purchased at a ***discount***. A discount is a price below a bond's ***face value***, whereby the amount paid the ***bondholder*** at maturity equals the original amount invested plus investment return. For example, the face amount of a bond is $1,000. However, because of economic factors, this particular bond sells for $875. If the bond investor pays $875 and waits until maturity to cash the bond, $125 ($1,000 - $875) is the profit received by the investor.

- A bond may also be purchased with a promise to repay the bondholder's investment plus a specified rate of interest (income). For instance, the bond costs $1,000 and it will pay 5.5% interest ($1,000 x 5.5%), or $55.

Perhaps you are familiar with United States savings bonds that are backed by the full faith and credit of the United States government. U.S. savings bonds, ***U.S. Treasury bills***, ***U.S. Treasury notes***, and ***U.S. Treasury bonds*** are considered a good risk. On the other hand, because of the low risk involved, the rate of return (interest) on U.S. securities can be low compared to other investments. And the income on bonds may not keep up with the rate of inflation.

In *Chapter 12 – Pyramid Basics: The Secret To Investing*, you will learn that usually (but not always) the greater the investment risk, the greater the potential for a higher rate of return. On the other hand, the lower the risk, the more probability for a lower rate of return.

This is not to say that people should not invest in bonds or other low-risk investments. On the contrary, it is important for a person's financial portfolio to be well **diversified**.

U.S. Savings Bonds can be purchased and redeemed electronically from a web-based system called TreasuryDirect.gov. TreasuryDirect.gov is the one and only place to electronically buy and redeem U.S. Savings Bonds. They also offer electronic sales and auctions of other U.S.-backed investments to the general public, financial professionals, and state and local governments. For more information, talk to your local banker or go to **TreasuryDirect.gov**.

Before moving on to the next chapter, remember:

- **A bond is a superior promise to repay a bondholder's investment plus interest.**

- **Bonds are generally considered conservative investments.**

- **Bonds help balance the risk of an investment portfolio.**

In *Chapter 8 – Stocks: The Place To Be*, we will study what powers and runs most corporations in the United States and the world … stocks!

CHAPTER 8

STOCKS

The Place To Be

In the United States and throughout the world, stocks rule! Tune in to the stock market shows on television to see what I mean. Today, many people are invested in the stock market. They are tracking stocks on their mobile devices and computers. The pace is hectic and exciting. What affects the companies of the world affects the world we live in, and vice versa.

You may be interested to know that shares of stock represent individual pieces of ownership in a corporation. When a company needs to raise money, it issues shares of stock for people to purchase through what is known as an *initial public offering (IPO)*. Initially, the price of stock is determined by the company. Once the stock has been traded (bought and sold) for a while, *supply and demand* takes over, placing a price per share value on the stock.

A company's *board of directors* may periodically declare that shareholders be paid a *dividend* (income) on each share of stock. I emphasize *may*. Dividends are not required to be paid to shareholders. Some companies rarely pay dividends, preferring to reinvest the profits earned back into the company to promote the company's growth, and some companies may not be able to afford to pay a dividend.

There are two kinds of stock.

- ***Common stock.*** Owners of common stock have the right to regularly vote for and elect a board of directors to manage the company's business. By electing a board of directors, owners of common stock have a say in the management of a corporation, yet don't have to be involved with the day-to-day activities of operating a business. Common stockholders also vote on corporate policy at annual meetings.

- ***Preferred stock.*** In the last chapter, we discussed how owners of bonds are paid before stock shareholders if the company goes bankrupt. The owners of ***preferred stock*** are next in line to be paid in the event of bankruptcy before common stockholders. Preferred stock is typically issued with a fixed dividend. This is an advantage, as the owners of preferred stock receive dividends before owners of common stock. Preferred stockholders generally do not have voting rights.

Like bonds, company stocks range in their degree of risk. Depending upon the financial stability of a company plus other factors, the stock can range from conservative to high-risk, or speculative.

Investing in stocks of newly formed companies is generally considered riskier than investing in companies that have been around for many years with good growth, earnings, and track records like Amazon, Meta, Alphabet (Google), Apple, Tesla, Microsoft, and Nvidia.

Companies investing large amounts of capital into new ventures with no earnings, such as a new artificial intelligence company or a small pharmaceutical company developing medicines for life-threatening diseases may be considered high-risk. While these companies may produce worthwhile products, the large debt they incur may pull down earnings and cash flow for years.

The stock of companies that have a track record of paying their stockholders dividends year after year may be a more conservative investment than the stock of a company that seldom if ever pays dividends. However, the dividend paying company may not have the rate of growth that a younger investor, with years until retirement, may want or need.

Sometimes newly formed companies generate large profits for stock market investors. Consider Google, Amazon, Walmart, and Microsoft. Initially, each of these companies was starting out in business, new and untested. Years ago, these companies' stock sold for significantly less than they do today. **Stock market investors make money by purchasing stock when the price is low and selling when the price is high.** By purchasing shares of stock when prices are low and selling when prices rise, investors can make large profits.

However, before investing in the stock market, I recommend that you read books, magazine articles, and company earnings reports, and watch stock market television programs. Some of my favorite books, magazines, and television programs are listed in the *Information Resources* at the back of this book.

Valuable company information can be found through market research conducted online, through stock brokerage firms, company websites, investor reports, financial newspapers and magazines, the business sections of many mainstream magazines and newspapers, and financial television programs. To understand the stock market, study a company's history, its future plans, its earnings, and its competition.

Before investing in a stock, research the company or companies that interest you. How do you make the decision to invest in a company? **Here are suggestions for selecting companies and their stocks. Try this exercise with a friend or classmate.**

1. Talk to stockbrokers and visit *stock brokerage* websites. Find someone who will provide you with information and talk to you about the stock market.

2. Select ten companies that interest you. Choose companies whose products you like or use. Pick companies that have been around for many years and some that are relatively new. Research these companies. Locate magazine articles about these companies in the **Reader's Guide To Periodical Literature.** Read the magazine articles, especially the ones in business magazines. Research the company online. Learn all you can about the company, what it produces, where it conducts business, its history, and how it is managed.

3.   **Choose five of the most interesting companies whose stock you'd like to buy.**

4.   **Limit your investment to an "on paper" investment.** Choose a *hypothetical* dollar amount to invest and invest an equal dollar amount in each stock. For example, you plan to hypothetically invest $10,000, you'll be investing $2,000 in each stock ($10,000 / 5 stocks).

5.   **On the same day, buy each stock at the price per share listed online.**

6.   **For three to six months track the changes in stock market prices in your notebook.**

7.   **Continue to study your individual stock companies.** Read information about the companies in sources like *Value Line Investment Survey*, *Standard & Poor's*, and *Morningstar*. Study company websites. This will help you understand why the stock price

fluctuates with each stock and will give you a much better insight to the world of the stock market.

The above exercise will teach you valuable lessons such as patience. The ups and downs of the stock market can be volatile. If the "paper money" had been your hard-earned cash, could you afford to lose a portion or all the money invested? Would you have the patience to ride out the lows and not panic and sell your stock when prices were down?

Stocks can be purchased through full-service **stock brokerage** firms and online brokers. This is the most common way for investors to buy individual stocks. Online brokers have made the process accessible and often commission-free.

If you decide to go with an online broker, such as Charles Schwab, Fidelity, or E*TRADE, pick the company that fits your needs regarding fees, research tools, and customer support. Afterwards, decide on an account type, such as a standard taxable brokerage account or a tax-advantaged retirement account like an IRA.

Online brokerage firms offer the ability to buy and sell stocks with no fees. Typical brokerage firms may charge a commission for advice. In addition to the stock price, there will be a sales charge to buy and a sales charge when you sell the stock. The sales charge will vary depending upon where you buy and sell the stock. Compare fees and services with discount and full-service stock brokerage firms.

Paying brokerage fees will not guarantee that you profit from your stock purchases. Whether you use a full-service stockbroker or invest online is a decision that should be based upon your level of knowledge. This knowledge should include the stock market in general, and the companies whose stocks you consider buying.

If you have an interest in a company, you should thoroughly do your homework researching the company, including its quarterly earnings reports and **annual report**s, and listening to conference calls. In addition, **research reports** are available from stock brokerage firms and online sources. Annual reports and research reports contain valuable information about a company including background information, company developments, and financial strength.

The Dow Jones Industrial Average is the most widely quoted

and popular measure of the stock market. The Dow Jones Industrial Average consists of thirty large publicly owned companies based in the United States. These stocks are listed on the **New York Stock Exchange**. Selected as representative of American industry, the thirty stocks are the **blue-chip** shares of large, well-known companies regarded as leaders in their industries and are widely held by individual and **institutional investors**.

If you plan to purchase individual stocks, my advice is to conduct your own research first. **Questions you need answered include:**

- **What is the company's history?**

- **What are future company plans?**

- **Is the company's stock price unusually high or low?**

- **How long have key company officials worked for the company?** Are any key people expected to leave the company?

- **Has a drastic change in management taken place?**

- **What is the company's dividend-paying history?** Has the company paid out too much in dividends, therefore limiting the amount of investment capital available?

- **What are consumer attitudes toward the company and its products?**

- **Do you like the company's products?**

- **Do your friends and family use the company's products?**

- **What is the company's competition?**

No one, I repeat, no one has a crystal ball when it comes to stock market performance. However, since the 1920s the returns generated by stocks have exceeded the returns received from fixed interest investments such as bank ***certificates of deposit (CDs)*** and bonds. Many investment gurus say, "The stock market is the place to be!"

When it comes to stocks remember:

- **The principle of supply and demand helps establish stock prices. That includes market demand and investor sentiment.**

- **Buying stock low and selling high is what generates**

profits for stock market investors.

- **Do complete and thorough research before investing.**

If you don't have time to individually research dozens of companies, read the next chapter and consider investing in mutual funds.

CHAPTER 9
MUTUAL FUNDS
Convenient Investing

For the *novice* investor, I recommend mutual funds for the following reasons:

- **Mutual funds are professionally managed by people with years of investment experience.**

- **By their very nature, mutual funds are diversified, a subject that will be covered in depth in *Chapter 12 – Pyramid Basics: The Secret To Investing*.**

An alternative to owning an individual company's stock is to own shares in a mutual fund.

A mutual fund is a group of stocks, bonds, or stocks and bonds managed by professional investment managers. When you own shares of a mutual fund, you own a portion of many companies, sometimes 50 to 100 or more!

By owning a mutual fund, an investor has the advantage of

professional fund management. Professional management means you don't spend hundreds of hours of your time researching individual companies. Mutual funds are managed by professional investment managers who do the research for you. These professional portfolio managers typically have many years of investment experience. **However, it is your responsibility to research the mutual fund before investing your money in the fund.**

By owning a mutual fund, you are typically diversified. You are investing in many companies, not placing all your money in only one company's stock. If your money is invested several different ways, the potential for risk is typically reduced. There are approximately 8,500 mutual funds in the United States at the time of printing.

Here are some important factors to consider before investing in a mutual fund:

1. **How long has the manager managed the fund?**

2. **Is the fund run by one individual or a panel of people?** Each approach has positive and negative aspects.

3. **What is the previous experience of the investment**

manager?

4.   **The mutual fund has at least a two or three-year history.**   While past results are no indication of future results, it is important to have a track record to examine.

5.   **How has the mutual fund performed?**

6.   **What are the mutual fund's management costs?**

The cost to purchase a mutual fund is generally the fund's *net asset value (NAV)* plus the cost of any sales charge. NAV is calculated by subtracting expenses incurred by a mutual fund from the value of a mutual fund's assets, and then dividing that amount by the number of shares in the mutual fund.

Sales charges pay the people who sell mutual funds. Some mutual funds have front-end sales charges. These are sales charges that are assessed when the mutual fund is purchased. Other mutual funds have what are referred to as back-end or contingent deferred sales charges. If you keep your money in the mutual fund for a required number of years, you will have limited or no sales charges. However, if you do redeem your mutual fund shares before the required number of years have passed, you will be charged the deferred sales charge, which usually declines the more years your money is invested.

An advantage to investing your money in mutual funds over individual stocks is the portfolio management. The mutual fund manager or group of managers track dozens to hundreds of companies. However, they don't work for free. Mutual fund managers are paid from management fees that are assessed against the mutual fund as expenses each year.

In addition, mutual funds charge **annual fees** that cover administrative costs, etc. Different mutual fund companies charge different percentage rates for annual fees and management fees.

Mutual funds are as diverse as the companies they represent. Mutual funds have different investment strategies. Investment strategy determines what types of companies a mutual fund will invest in. Mutual funds may be growth, income, growth and income, international, bonds, foreign, large-cap, small-cap, **socially responsible**, or aggressive growth-oriented.

Mutual fund managers invest in the stock of companies that follow their investment strategies. If a fund has an aggressive growth strategy, money of the fund may be invested in the stock of companies that are emerging at the time. Emerging companies include high technology companies that reinvest most of their profits back into the company instead of paying the shareholders any dividends.

Long-term investing in a mutual fund is recommended–at least four to five years, since most mutual funds have sales charges, whether front-end or contingent deferred.

Mutual fund share values will fluctuate. Invest for the long term. Otherwise, you might need to sell at a time when the stock market is low and your mutual fund value has declined. Selling at the wrong time could result in a financial loss to you.

Before purchasing a mutual fund, you should be provided a ***prospectus*** by the mutual fund company or its representative salesperson. A mutual fund prospectus includes the investment strategy, types of companies the fund invests in, expenses and fees, and management ***philosophy***.

There are approximately 8,500 mutual funds in the United States. Mutual fund companies have several to hundreds of separate funds that offer the investor any type of investment strategy or philosophy possible. Like stock prices, the share price of a mutual fund can be tracked online.

Here are tips for mutual fund investments:

1.   **Read the prospectus.**

2.   **Ask the mutual fund's sales representative lots of questions.** If the sales representative won't answer your questions, this probably isn't a mutual fund where you want to invest your hard-earned money.

3.   **Talk to people you trust.** Ask what mutual funds they recommend. Who are their financial representatives?

4.   **Read articles in financial magazines and newspapers about the fund.** You will see a list of some of these publications at the end of this book. Conduct research online.

5.   **Watch financial and investment television programs.**

6.   **Don't get hooked by the *flavor of the month*.** Research any mutual fund you consider buying.

7.   **Make your investment decisions based upon sound research, investigation, and thought.**

8.   Work with a mutual fund representative you like and respect.

9.   Invest for the long-term.

In review:

- Mutual funds invest in the stock of dozens to hundreds of companies.

- Mutual funds are professionally managed.

- Select a mutual fund based upon the fund's investment strategy and your own investment needs.

Now that we've covered several different investment options, in *Chapter 10* we will explore some ways to protect your ***assets***.

CHAPTER 10

INSURANCE

Protect Your Assets

I bet the type of insurance you have heard the most about is car insurance. For the average teen, automobile insurance is expensive, so you may have a negative opinion of insurance.

We've covered automobile insurance in the chapter on budgets. In this chapter, we will discuss life insurance—what it does and how it works.

Life insurance is usually purchased in the event someone dies whose income is necessary for the survival of a family.

Premiums are payments made for life insurance. They are paid monthly, quarterly, semi-annually, or annually.

Whole life insurance policies are a type of life insurance that accumulates ***cash value*** as premiums are paid over the years. Whole life insurance premiums typically stay the same year after year. As cash value grows, it can be used by the owner of the insurance policy to help purchase a home, pay for college, or finance retirement. If the cash value is not depleted below the level that pays for the life insurance, the policy stays in force. Therefore, the life insurance protection stays in effect.

Term life insurance is a type of life insurance that does not accumulate cash value. Term life insurance premiums for young people are lower than whole life insurance premiums. As the ***insured*** ages, the cost of premiums may increase, making term insurance prohibitively expensive later in life.

Here are some tips for selecting an insurance company:

1. **Talk to friends, relatives, and people whose opinions you respect.** Ask them to recommend an insurance agent and insurance company.

2. **Research the life insurance company.**

3. **Has the company existed a long time?** Fifty years or more indicates that a company is financially strong, has weathered the test of time, and may be around for another fifty years.

4. **Does the life insurance company have a good reputation and a good record of paying *claims*?** How is the

company rated? You can learn the answer to this question by researching reports from insurance reporting services such as A.M. Best.

Life insurance can be purchased with investment options that resemble mutual funds. **When purchasing life insurance with investment options:**

- **Read the prospectus.** It's a long read, so allow plenty of time to study the prospectus.

- **Study the track record and return history of the investment options.** How long has it been in existence? How has it performed?

- **What are the costs of the policy and the investment options?**

- **Diversify your investment options like you would any other type of investment.** If your other investments are fixed interest or low-risk, you may want to balance your portfolio by being moderately or slightly aggressive in your investment approach. Or you may want to invest in several options. For instance, 25% fixed, 25% bonds, 25% stocks, and 25% aggressive investments.

When interest rates are low, stocks often do well. The opposite is also true. In other words, when the stock market is down, interest rates may be high and give you a good return in fixed accounts. Historically the United States has experienced cycles of a booming stock market with low interest rates versus a declining stock market with higher interest rates.

In review, some important life insurance points include:

- **Insurance protects the financial assets and earning power of a wage earner.**

- **The cost of purchasing life insurance increases as a person grows older.**

- **For young adults, term life insurance premiums are lower than whole life insurance premiums.**

- **Whole life insurance provides cash values that can be used to pay for college, a home, or retirement.**

- **Life insurance can be purchased with investment**

options.

After all this talk about bonds, stocks, mutual funds, and insurance, we'll now explore one of the biggest reasons to save and invest today—the American dream—a home!

CHAPTER 11

REAL ESTATE

The American Dream

Owning your own home (real estate) is the American dream! Consider it this way, everyone needs a place to live … why not own it?

Most homes can be purchased with approximately a 20% down payment (the amount of cash you pay toward the sale price) and financing the remaining balance with a **mortgage**. A mortgage entitles a buyer to make monthly payments for the next ten, twenty, or thirty years at a fixed or variable rate of interest, instead of paying all cash for a house, which most people cannot afford.

According to the National Association of Realtors®, as of September 2025, the median sale price of an existing home in the United States was $415,200. This price was a 2.1% increase from September 2024. Compare $415,200 to $188,900, the average price of an existing home in January 2017.

Based on a sale price of $415,200, a 20% down payment for the average priced home today would equal $83,040.

In addition to **conventional bank mortgage** home loans, there are government-backed programs like those available from the Federal Home Administration (FHA) and the Veterans Administration (VA). These programs can enable a home buyer to purchase a home with a much smaller down payment than a conventional bank mortgage.

There are also various loan programs, such as first-time homebuyer programs, which require as little as 0% to 5% down payment. Talk to a loan officer or mortgage lender at your local bank, savings and loan association, credit union, or mortgage company to learn what programs exist in your area.

Some people who want to sell their homes will owner-finance. This means the buyer makes monthly payments to the seller instead of a bank. The seller retains title (ownership) of the house until the loan is paid off.

Sometimes an ***owner-financed*** real estate transaction may involve more lenient financing terms. Reasons a home seller would owner-finance are a slow selling real estate market, the property owner wants the income from the loan interest, or the owner wants to defer **capital gains taxes**.

When a mortgage loan is paid off, you own the property free and clear.

When a lender considers an application for a home loan, they will look for the following:

1. **The ability of the buyer to repay the loan.**

2. **Good credit of the buyer.**

3. **Delinquent or late payments on previous loans.**

4. **Bankruptcies if any.**

5. **A proportionate amount of annual income to the sale price of the house.** A rule of thumb is the sale price should be no more than 2.5 times your total annual income. For instance, if your income is $75,000 per year, the sale price of your home should be no more than $187,500 ($75,000 x 2.5). With the average home costing $415,200, it will take time to find a home that meets your needs in today's real estate market. The current high price of houses and the 2.5 rule of thumb explains why the income of two parents is needed

Rich!

today to pay for many families' housing needs.

6. A proportionate amount of home mortgage payment to total income. A home mortgage payment should not exceed 28% of a person's gross monthly income. For instance, if your monthly income is $6,250 per month ($75,000 annually), your monthly house payment should not exceed $1,750 per month ($6,250 x 28%).

7. A proportionate amount of monthly debt payments and home mortgage to total income. A person's monthly debt payments and house payment combined should not exceed approximately 36% of his or her gross monthly salary. For instance, if your monthly income is $6,250, your monthly debts including house payment should not exceed $2,250 per month ($6,250 x 36%).

If a person can't meet the above criteria, they may not be able to purchase a home through a banking institution. This person must make a larger down payment or find a less expensive house to purchase. More reason to read *Chapter 13 – Higher Education: Your Key to the Future*, to help you get the highest paying job possible!

If a lender will make a disproportionately high loan compared to your income, you should decline the loan. Remember, it's easier to get into debt than to get out of debt.

I encourage people to keep their house payments as low as possible and have as much ***equity*** in the home as possible. A low house payment and more equity can be accomplished by making a larger down payment, purchasing a ***fixer-upper***, buying a less expensive house, or doubling up on payments as your income increases.

There is no guarantee what life will bring our way. If it takes two people working in a family to make a house payment and one partner gets laid off from work, it can be difficult to make a home mortgage payment. That's why I recommend as low a house payment as possible *and* paying that mortgage down as soon as possible.

Mortgage payments usually are made for ten, twenty, or thirty years. While a longer payback term such as thirty years can make for the lowest monthly payment, it can triple the amount of interest, and thus the amount of money you pay for the house in the long run. I generally recommend a payback period of ten to twenty years.

Tips for buying a house:

1. **Location, location, location.** That is the secret of home buying. Purchase a home in the best area you can afford.

2. **Find a real estate agent you like and trust.** Real estate agents typically work on a commission basis. This means they don't get paid until the house sale closes *escrow*. Once you select an agent, respect that person's time and be loyal.

3. **Choose a house with a price tag you can afford.**

4. **Unless you are skilled in the construction trades or have a very close friend or relative who is** … stay away from fixer-uppers. A *fixer-upper* could cause more dollars being invested in the house than it's worth.

5. **Buy a house that's compatible with the neighborhood.** This means your house is similar to other houses in the neighborhood. Do not purchase a home that is over-improved for the neighborhood. An example of over-improvement would be a home with four bedrooms and two bathrooms located in a neighborhood where the homes are two bedrooms with one bathroom. The value of a superior house tends to be pulled downward by the influence of the smaller, less expensive houses.

However, sometimes the value of a smaller, less expensive house will be pulled upward by the influence of larger, more expensive homes in the neighborhood. This could be a good buying opportunity.

6. A *duplex house* may also be a good buying opportunity. You live in one unit and rent the other side to a tenant. Thus, your mortgage could partially be paid by your tenant.

Owning your own home is an important step to your financial future. It may be years before you are ready to take this step. However, owning a home is a very worthwhile long-term goal.

In review:

- **A down payment is the amount of money that a home buyer pays toward the purchase price of a home.**

- **A mortgage allows a home buyer to make monthly payments toward the purchase of a home.**

- **Choose a house with a sale price you can afford.**

- **Select a house that's compatible with the neighborhood.**

Now that we have discussed several investment options, read *Chapter 12 – Pyramid Basics: The Secret To Investing*, to learn how to allocate your investment dollars to help reduce investment risk.

CHAPTER 12

PYRAMID BASICS

The Secret To Investing

Many financial advisors use the pyramid when advising their investment and estate planning clients. I recommend using the pyramid to structure your ***investment portfolio***. The pyramid helps create a snapshot of a person's finances.

Draw a large pyramid on a page in your notebook. Start at the bottom of the pyramid and draw a line across the pyramid, approximately one-third of the way up from the bottom. Next draw a line approximately two-thirds of the way up from the bottom. Now draw a third line almost at the very top of the pyramid, so that a very small triangle is left. There should now be four sections in your pyramid.

The bottom portion of the pyramid is considered the base. You should have a solid financial base to build a strong financial future. A good financial base is premised on fixed

interest and guaranteed principal investments.

Fixed interest and guaranteed *principal* investments include savings accounts, checking accounts, bank certificates of deposit, U.S. savings bonds, and U.S. Treasury bills. In other words, there is a high probability that the money you invest will be returned to you.

Insurance protection, whether it is for a car, home, medical, *disability*, or life insurance, also falls within the base of the pyramid.

Money invested in the bottom portion of the pyramid is conservative investment. All of us need some conservative investments.

Notice that as you move upward on the pyramid, the shape of the pyramid becomes narrower. The shape of the pyramid illustrates that as the potential for return increases, the potential for loss also increases. Therefore, you may want to limit the amounts you invest in risky areas.

Now move upward to the next portion of the pyramid. This section is for moderate investments. Moderate investments may include bonds, income stocks, and income mutual funds. Depending upon the strength of the company, moderate investments may also include some growth stocks and growth mutual funds. Also, a home where you reside would also fall within this portion of the pyramid.

Now move upward to the next portion of the pyramid. This section is for aggressive investments. Aggressive stock investments may not pay dividends to investors. The company may prefer to reinvest profits back into the company so it may grow.

Depending upon the quality of bonds and stocks, they can be conservative, moderate, or even aggressive, investments. For instance, corporate bonds of a company with a poor record of paying interest on its bonds may be considered an aggressive investment.

Aggressive investments are considered riskier than fixed and moderate investments, but have the potential for greater return. Aggressive investments may include the stocks, bonds, or mutual funds of newly formed companies, young companies, technology and AI companies.

Next move into the small triangle at the very top of the pyramid. This is known as the area of high-risk investments. High-risk investments have the potential for large profits. However, the greatest chance of losing some, or all, of your original investment is in the high-risk area.

Loss of investment capital is possible with *all* investments, except guaranteed principal investments located in the bottom section of the pyramid. With high-risk investments, the potential for principal loss is *very* high. As with all investments, when investing in the high-risk area, the investor should thoroughly conduct research and be very knowledgeable.

High-risk investments include speculative stocks, **junk bonds** (below investment grade bonds), limited partnerships, rare coins, stamps, **commodities**, and gold and silver bullion. While I do not discourage all high-risk investments, I do urge investor knowledgeability and relatively small dollar amounts invested in this area. I also recommend sufficient investments in the other levels of the pyramid before venturing into the high-risk category.

There are no cut-and-dried rules to investing. However, the most tried and true method is diversification, also known as **asset allocation**. Diversification is the process of investing in various sections of the pyramid. If you spread your investment dollars over the different investment categories of the pyramid, the potential for loss is reduced.

In theory, not all investments thrive at once and not all investments decline at the same time. For instance, when growth stocks are up in value, then bonds may be down in value. By allocating your investment dollars into different sections of the pyramid, balance will be achieved and the potential for loss is reduced.

The style of diversification that an investor selects depends upon the individual investor. People who are near retirement risk the loss of needed cash if their investments are too aggressive. If a person is dependent upon the income from investments to maintain their standard of living, a conservative to moderate approach to investing should be considered.

However, being overly conservative today may not be well advised due to inflation and taxes. If a retired person lives for 20 to 30 more years after retiring and the cost of goods and services continues to inflate (rise) at an annual rate of 3% inflation, after 15 years that individual's cost of living has increased by approximately

56%! If this individual's income does not increase, he or she may face old age with not enough money at a time when life should be free of worries.

Even more reason to start saving and investing at your age. Remember in *Chapter 3 – Saving & Investing: Time Is On Your Side*, how our $2,000 investment grew to over $148,500? You will be amazed how much your investments can accumulate and grow over years.

For a teenager, with the luxury of time to withstand the ups and downs of the stock market, you can afford moderate or aggressive investments. This is an advantage over someone who waits until late in life to start investing.

A hybrid form of diversification is a method of investing called **dollar-cost averaging**. Instead of investing all your money at the same time, it's more practical to dollar-cost average. The practice of dollar-cost averaging is a systematic method of contributing a fixed dollar amount or percentage of your income to an investment on a regular basis, say monthly.

For instance, if you decide to invest $50 per month in ABC Mutual Fund, one month your $50 may buy 2 mutual fund shares when the price per share is $25 per share. However, a month or two later, perhaps the mutual fund is down in price, to say $20 per share; then your $50 will buy 2½ shares. Therefore, you are buying more shares when prices are low and fewer shares when prices are high. By dollar-cost averaging, your investment risk is reduced. Dollar-cost averaging takes the emotion out of investing and implements a logical plan of investment that's well suited for long-term goals.

As you make investment decisions remember:

- **Diversification of your investments may include conservative, moderate, aggressive, and high-risk investments.**

- **Diversify your *investment portfolio* to suit your risk tolerance.**

- **Dollar-cost average your investment dollars to help reduce risk.**

Next, let's explore one of the best reasons to invest today, higher education.

CHAPTER 13
HIGHER EDUCATION
Your Key To The Future

In my opinion, this is the most important chapter in this book. Life for you in the competitive world of the 21st century will require the best education and skills possible. Higher education beyond high school will be more important than ever to compete for the best careers that will ensure a lifestyle to which you want to become accustomed!

Higher education will widen your horizons. Higher education will be significant in the workplace of the 21st century. Specialized and advanced educational degrees and certifications will be vital to a sound financial future.

Higher education includes vocational/technical schools, community colleges, public and private colleges and universities, and medical, dental, and law schools.

Obtaining a higher education is a goal you should pursue wholeheartedly. Mandatory college courses required the first two years will open doors to parts of the world you've never visited. In college, you will establish friendships that can last a lifetime. The friends you eat lunch with in the student union and cram for exams late into the night will be contacts and business associates who have connections to the careers and jobs you desire.

Higher education options include:

1.   **Vocational and Technical Schools.**   Many good professions do not require a four-year degree. The education for non-degree occupations, which includes white and blue-collar jobs, can be obtained through vocational and technical schools. These professions require specialized education that is obtained through accredited courses with substantially less time and expense.

2.   **Community Colleges.** This is a higher education option (a two-year postsecondary institution) that offers opportunities for educational enrichment at more affordable prices. Community colleges often are local and state supported. By attending local community colleges, students can begin the pursuit of higher education and keep expenses nominal by living at home.

3.   **State Colleges and Universities.** These institutions of

higher learning offer four years of education at reasonable rates. Master's and doctor's degrees are also offered at these schools.

4. Private Universities. These schools generally are not *subsidized* by taxpayer money, and therefore, cost more to attend. Master's and doctor's degrees may be offered at these schools.

5. Medical, Dental and Law Schools. These schools may be part of a university system or an entirely separate school. These schools are expensive.

The cost of a higher education is a primary consideration when deciding to attend college. In fact, four years or more of additional education can be very expensive.

Presently tuition and fees for in-state students at two-year public colleges average $4,050 per year. For the 2024-2025 academic year, the average cost of tuition and fees at public four-year colleges is $11,610 for in-state students and $30,780 for out-of-state students. The average yearly cost of tuition and fees for a four-year private college is approximately $39,400 to $41,540.

The costs for students wanting to obtain a master's or doctorate degree, or attend law, dental, or medical school are higher. For instance, the average yearly tuition for law school is around $30,000 for in-state students, over $40,000 for out-of-state students, and approximately $46,029 for private law schools.

Medical school tuition for the 2024-2025 academic year varies by institution type, with averages around $59,720 or higher for a typical year. These tuition costs are average figures, and the actual cost can vary significantly depending on the state and resident status.

The tuition figures do not include expenses like room and board. Therefore, you must also consider costs for room and board and books and supplies. While room and board costs vary throughout the country, the average yearly cost of room and board for a four-year public college is approximately $12,639. The average yearly room and board cost for a four-year private college is approximately $15,250. Room and board for the first year of medical school were estimated to be $27,200 by the Association of American Medical Colleges (AAMC). Room and board costs typically include both housing accommodations and a meal plan.

The cost of four to ten years of higher education amounts to staggering sums. However, tuition costs may be lowered for many students through grants, scholarships, and other financial aid. Appreciate the fact that planning early is a necessity and requires patience.

The financing of your advanced education is no different than saving for any other financial investment. Financing a higher education requires setting goals, discipline, and following through with your goals.

Tips for financing your higher education:

- **Set aside as much as possible for college on a regular basis.** The sooner the better. Follow the suggestions in *Chapter 4 – Making A Budget* to help you achieve your college savings goals.

- **Suggest relatives contribute to a 529 Plan for you.** A 529 plan is a tax-advantage investment account designed to help families save for education expenses, from kindergarten through graduate school. Contributions grow tax-deferred, and withdrawals for qualified educational expenses are tax-free at the federal level and, in many cases, at the state level as well.

- **What type of higher education do you want to attend—** vocational and technical schools, community colleges, public or private colleges, medical or law schools?

- **What schools interest you?** Obtain school information online, from high school guidance counselors, the library, and individual schools. Select six schools to explore.

- **Visit the schools as early as possible.** Contact the school's admissions office to schedule a visit to the campus. During your visit, tour school departments and speak with professors and financial aid officers. Ask lots of questions. These visits will help determine which schools you prefer.

- **During school visits, learn the cost of tuition, room, board, books, and supplies per year.** Multiply the annual cost by the number of years you plan to attend school. This will be the approximate cost of attending post-secondary school before inflation.

- **Attend community college for two years to save money.** Afterwards, transfer to a state-subsidized public university.

- **In-state tuition for resident students is less than attending college as a non-resident.** Attend a school in a state where you are a resident. Residency requirements are important and vary at different schools. Talk to a school counselor to determine your residency status.

- **Know deadline dates and application fees for each school you want to attend.**

- **Remember our discussion of inflation in *Chapter 6 – Taxes & Inflation*?** Inflation can also adversely affect the cost of a higher education. If you are several years away from attending college, factor in the cost of inflation.

Inflation rates for college tuition, room and board have varied over the years. For the 2025-2026 academic year, the inflation rate for public colleges ranged from 3.3% for in-state and 3.7% for out-of-state students. Private colleges ranged from 3.3% to 3.9%. And some elite private institutions reported even higher increases, up to 4.2% or more.

If you do not attend college for four more years, the cost of a higher education could increase by more than 20% (4 years @ 5% inflation) by the time you're ready to attend. Inflation can add tremendously to college costs and must be factored into any college budget. **Use the following College Cost Worksheet and Inflation Factor tables to determine your college costs.**

<u>College Cost Worksheet</u>

1. **Number of years until college.**

2. **Current yearly cost of your college.**

3. **Multiply yearly cost by inflation factor (see below).**

4. **Yearly college cost.**

5. **Multiply by number of years you plan to attend.**

6. **Your estimated future college cost.**

INFLATION FACTORS

Years Until College	4%	6%	8%
1	1.04	1.06	1.08
2	1.08	1.12	1.17
3	1.12	1.19	1.26
4	1.17	1.26	1.36
5	1.22	1.34	1.47
6	1.27	1.42	1.59
7	1.32	1.50	1.71
8	1.37	1.59	1.85
9	1.42	1.69	2.00
10	1.48	1.79	2.16

It's important to plan early for the financing of your higher education. However, even the best-laid plans can be derailed by escalating college expenses. Even with early planning, summer jobs, investments, and help from relatives, the money necessary to finance your college education simply may not be available to embark on your freshman year. This is when financial aid becomes important.

Obtaining financial aid requires research, patience, and creativity. Financial aid may appear elusive. Don't get discouraged. Be positive! There are more grants and scholarships available than you thought possible.

The remainder of this chapter is devoted to learning how to pay for your higher education with financial aid. Your journey may not be easy. Nevertheless, if you are determined to make a success of your life, there are ways available to get the education you desire.

Student financial aid includes:

- **Grants are financial aid that do not require repayment.**

- **Scholarships do not require repayment dollar for dollar.** However, this type of financial aid might require an after-graduation commitment of service or employment.

- **Loans.** Many students finance their higher education either partially or completely with student loans. Loans are required to be paid back. Repayment usually does not begin until after graduation.

- **Work-Study is a federal financial aid program that provides part-time jobs for students with financial need,** allowing them to earn money to help pay for college expenses while gaining work experience. The jobs can be located on-campus (like in a library or dining hall) or off-campus with public agencies or non-profit organizations.

Since loans must be repaid, obtaining as much financial aid as possible through grants and scholarships is advisable. Competition for financial aid is tough for grants and scholarships. There are limited dollars available for these programs.

Therefore, it is essential to apply to your schools and submit financial aid applications well before deadlines. If you expect to attend school in the fall, don't postpone applying for financial aid until a month or two before school begins.

Apply for financial aid nearly a year before you plan to attend college or early in your senior year of high school. Remember deadlines vary at different schools.

To obtain financial aid from federal programs available across the United States, you first must file the **Free Application for Federal Student Aid (FAFSA).** This application is available at the Federal Student Aid website, **studentaid.gov**.

By completing the FAFSA, you have an opportunity to obtain financial assistance from a variety of sources. Following is a list of Federal Student Financial Aid Programs available with a brief description of each.

1.   **Federal Pell Grants.** A Federal Pell Grant does not have to be repaid and is available to students who are undergraduates. The 2025-2026 Pell Grant award is up to $7,395, depending on your circumstances. Obtaining a Federal Pell Grant and how much you receive depends upon:

- **Your financial need.**

- **Your cost to attend school.**

- **Your status as a full-time or part-time student.**

- **Your plans to attend school for a full academic year or less.**

2. **Federal Supplemental Educational Opportunity Grants** (FSEOG) are for undergraduate students with exceptional financial need. Students who receive Pell Grants and have the most financial need will receive FSEOGs first. Funding is limited, and not all schools participate. The FSEOG is administered by your school's financial aid office, so you should check with them to see if it's available. Grant awards under this program range from $100 to $4,000 per year depending on your financial need, when you apply,

the amount of other aid you receive, and the availability of funds at your school.

3. **Teacher Education Assistance for College and Higher Education (TEACH) Grants** require you to take certain kinds of classes to receive the grant, and then teach within certain requirement fields to keep the grant from turning into a loan. TEACH provides grants up to $4,000 per year for full-time students.

4. **Iraq and Afghanistan Service Grants** are eligible to students based upon Pell Grant criteria and death of parent or guardian while serving as a member of the U.S. Armed Forces in Iraq or Afghanistan after the events of 9/11.

5. **Federal Work Study (FWS)** provides part-time employment for students with financial need. Students earn the federal minimum wage or higher. Work study jobs are located at school campuses, federal, state or local public agencies, private nonprofit organizations and for-profit organizations.

6. **Direct Subsidized Loans** are for eligible undergraduate students with financial need, where the U.S. Department of Education pays the interest while the student is in school at least half-

time, during the grace period, and during deferment.

7. **Direct Unsubsidized Loans** are available to undergraduate, graduate, and professional students regardless of financial need, where the borrower is responsible for all interest.

8. **Direct PLUS Loans** are for graduate or professional students and parents of dependent undergraduates, not based on financial need but requiring a credit check, and the borrower is responsible for all interest.

9. **Direct Consolidation Loans** allow combining multiple eligible federal student loans into a single loan.

In addition to federal financial aid programs, there are other sources of student aid available. These financial aid programs include:

- **State Scholarships** available through individual states may include teaching scholarships, nursing scholarships and ethnic/minority scholarships. State scholarships are based on scholastic merit, SAT and ACT scores, as well as financial need. This type of scholarship may entail an after-graduation commitment to a stated vocation. To learn about state scholarships available in your state of residence, check online at your state's higher education agency, and contact the financial aid office at the schools you consider attending.

- **Institutional grants.** Many colleges and universities offer their own grants, usually based on financial need. You can be considered for these grants by filling out the FAFSA and, in some cases, a separate application required by the school.

- **Specialized Field of Study.** If you intend to go into a specialized field, (for example engineering), scholarship monies may be available through local companies or trade organizations to help curtail the high costs of pursuing certain occupations. However, these types of scholarships may only be available to college juniors and seniors. Check online or contact your school's financial aid office to learn details.

- **National Scholarships** can be merit-based, need-based, or focused on specific fields of study, leadership, or demographic groups. The public library, school financial aid offices, and the web are good sources of information about national scholarships.

- **ROTC Scholarships.** Air Force, Army, and Naval Reserve Officers Training Corps programs provide scholarship and professional opportunities for students. These programs may pay for tuition, fees, books, supplies, and provide a monthly tax-free stipend. Participants take ROTC courses as they pursue their university degrees. After graduating and completing ROTC requirements, participants then receive commissions and begin their service in their chosen branch of the armed forces.

- **Scholarship Searches.** By conducting scholarship searches online, at the college of your choice, or paying a fee to a reputable scholarship search company, you may discover scholarship or loan funds offered by agencies or companies located outside of your city or state. Factors such as your academic goals, your parents' profession, place of residence, or status as a veteran may make you eligible for scholarships or low interest loans.

Most students are eligible to receive federal financial aid to assist with college or vocational school costs. Even though your income, including your parents, is considered, it does not automatically prevent you from receiving federal student aid.

To be eligible for one or more of the above-mentioned federal programs you must:

- Be a U.S. citizen or an eligible noncitizen with a valid Social Security number.

- Have a high school diploma or a GED.

- Be enrolled or accepted for enrollment as a student in an eligible degree or certificate program.

- Demonstrate financial need for need-based aid programs.

- Not be in default on a federal student loan and do not owe a refund on a federal grant.

- Use federal student aid only for educational purposes.

- Maintain satisfactory academic progress.

- Comply with Selective Service registration.

To begin the financial aid process, go to the Federal Student Aid website: **studentaid.gov**, and complete the **Free Application for**

Federal Student Aid (FAFSA).

The FAFSA website contains extensive information about the application process. First, before completing the FAFSA application, you will need to create a StudentAid.gov account.

To start the online FAFSA form, select "Start New Form." You'll be taken to the "Log In" page to enter your account username and password. After logging in, you'll be given the option to select your applicable role to fill out the FAFSA form: "Student" or "Parent." You (the student) should select "Student." If a parent wants to start their dependent child's FAFSA form, they should select the "Parent" option.

Some of the important information/documents you will need to provide for your FAFSA application includes:

1. Your dependent or ***independent*** student status.

2. Personal information. Your name, legal address, Social Security number (if you don't have a Social Security number, apply for one), parent's Social Security numbers if you are a dependent student, and your driver's license number.

3. Federal tax information or tax returns for you and parents if

you are a dependent student.

4. Records of untaxed income, such as interest income, child support, etc.

5. Asset information for student and parents. Assets include cash, savings, and checking accounts. The market value of real estate and other investments and the amount of debt owed. Assets also include stocks and bonds, and mutual funds.

6. List colleges and vocational/technical schools. You must list at least one college or vocational school to receive your information. It is advisable to list as many as six.

7. Sign your FAFSA application electronically.

8. Make a copy of your FAFSA application for your records.

As you complete the FAFSA form, follow the prompts, use the "Search" button, and the "Help" function as needed, or contact the financial aid office at the school you plan to attend. Once the application has been completed, check your email for updates.

Once your form is processed, you'll receive a copy of your FAFSA Submission Summary, which summarizes the information you provided on your FAFSA form. Review your FAFSA

Submission Summary and make sure all of the information is complete and accurate.

Once your FAFSA form is processed, it is sent to the schools you listed on your FAFSA form. Those schools are responsible for creating your aid offer and disbursing your financial aid. However, listing a college or vocational school on your FAFSA form is generally not sufficient to receive aid at that school, as most schools do not create aid packages for applicants until they are admitted to the school.

Contact the financial aid office at the school you plan to attend to find out if there are additional requirements for receiving financial aid and to learn more about the process of applying for aid to that school.

The timing of the aid offer varies from school to school. It depends on when you apply and how the school prefers to schedule awarding of aid. **Therefore, complete your FAFSA as early as possible.**

You may accept or reject the award offered. If you decide not to attend a school, be responsible and contact their financial aid office to inform them of your decision so another deserving student will receive financial aid instead.

College and vocational school scholarship tips include:

1. Type all applications, letters, questionnaires, essays and any other information that is part of the application for financial aid.

2. Carefully read all application materials before you submit your application. Be sure there are no typographical errors, obvious corrections, or messy or crumpled papers if submitted through the mail.

3. Have a trusted friend, teacher, or relative proofread your scholarship application for errors before the application is sent.

4. Attend scholarship workshops and talk to people who have received scholarships. Learn what individual scholarship winners did to receive their awards.

A lot of information is needed to properly fill out financial aid applications. Don't ***procrastinate*** and expect to complete the application at the last minute. The application will take time, so start early.

Whatever amount of time involved, the financial aid application process is extremely important. After all, financial aid could make the difference between obtaining a higher education or not.

Remember one vital rule when searching for financial aid:

- **Consider all sources ... leave no stone unturned.**

Also, if you don't qualify for a specific type of financial aid your freshman year, you may be eligible in the next year or two. Once you are over the hurdle of your freshman and sophomore years, there should be more opportunities for financial aid from departmental and specialized field of study sources.

If you are not able to immediately attend college after high school, don't despair. Time is on your side! If need be, take a year or two off to save more money. Just don't postpone your decision to pursue higher education too long. Being out of school too long is not in your best interest. You get out of the practice of being a student, and sometimes procrastination leads to permanent neglect. An alternative could be to attend school part-time for a year or two, and still maintain a full-time job.

There should be no excuse for indefinitely postponing a higher education. Search and apply for the grant, scholarship, work study, and loan programs that are available.

Obtaining a higher education may not be easy. No one in this country is guaranteed a higher education. Therefore, it requires your determination, hard work, and energy.

There's going to be a lot of competition in the 21st century. Those who have knowledge will hold the keys to the future! If you are willing to work hard and smart, you can get that education.

In summary:

- **A higher education is the ticket to a successful future.**

- **If you're several years away from college, inflation could increase costs by the time you're ready to attend.**

- **Visit the schools you're interested in attending a year or two before.**

- **There are many sources of financial aid for a higher education; be persistent and creative.**

Now that we've covered higher education, we'll discuss in *Chapter*

14 what hopefully happens after you graduate.

CHAPTER 14

JOBS

Do What You Enjoy

Whether you are looking for a job now or when you graduate from vocational school or college, there are certain steps to take when job hunting.

The following are hints and suggestions for finding the job of your dreams!

- **The best jobs are not always found online or in newspapers.** While these resources are a place to start, consider other alternatives.

- **Contact companies where you'd like to work.** Asking for the name of the person who does the hiring is a good job hunting technique. Follow up by calling that person and asking for a job interview.

- **Tell everyone you know that you're looking for a job.** That includes parents, relatives, friends of your parents, teachers, coaches, guidance counselors, ministers, your friends' parents, and people where you shop or do business. In other words, everyone you know should know you're looking for a job. **Networking** is an excellent way to land a good job. This way no source goes unexplored.

- **States and cities have job service centers where you can search for jobs online or in person.** Listings change daily or weekly so check back often. Be persistent. It will take time. The staff at a job service center will learn that you are serious and be more likely to remember you and your skills when they receive a job order.

- **Temp agencies can be a gateway to a permanent position.** Register with a temp agency and tackle small part-time jobs. A potential employer has an opportunity to see you work and may offer you a full-time job!

- Search online for jobs. Many websites and search engines specialize in employment opportunities. You can search by job category and location.

Rich!

- **Social networking.** LinkedIn is a good source for establishing a business profile and networking for career opportunities. Use a professional-looking photo. List your skills in an easy-to-read format. Keep your skills current and update as needed. Compare business profiles in the industry you wish to work. Hire a professional to write your profile, or ask for help from a librarian or teacher.

Throughout your job search, be prepared to hear "No" and don't be discouraged. Also, be prepared for "Yes." When you do get a "Yes" for a job interview, you will need to prepare.

Interviews, online or in person, are very important to getting a job. Your appearance, your behavior, and your ability to communicate are important factors to consider before and during an interview. You only have one chance to make a first impression!

Consider going for a job interview like performing in a theater play. You must prepare for the interview. By preparing what you say, how you respond to questions, and what questions you ask about the job, you will be more relaxed during the interview.

Begin your preparation for the interview by writing an

"elevator pitch". In a few sentences, briefly summarize your qualifications, what skills you would bring to the job, why you want the job, and why you would be great for the position.

In addition, write down some questions for the employer. These will include:

- **What are the job responsibilities?**

- **What does the employer expect from the person hired?**

- **To whom do you report?**

- **What are the hours?**

- **What is the salary?**

- **What are the benefits?** Benefits may include medical insurance, sick leave pay, and vacation time.

Before going to an interview, make a list of the jobs and responsibilities you have held in the past. If you have never held a job before, you can include classes you've attended, after-school activities, and references.

References are a list of people that your prospective employer may contact to learn more about you. A potential employer may ask a reference about your behavior, your positive and negative characteristics, and your willingness to be responsible and on time.

Always ask references for permission to use their names. If you have any questions that a person may not vouch for you, don't use that person as a reference. Along with your reference names, include job title, company name, email address, and telephone number. List at least two or three references. As your job and life experiences grow, you'll update and add to your list of references.

Practice makes perfect. With your list of questions, answers, and statements to the employer, stand in front of a mirror. Look yourself right in the eye, recite your "elevator pitch", ask your questions and recite your answers into the mirror. Don't be discouraged if you're not comfortable or you forget what to say. Simply practice over and over again in front of the mirror.

Remember to smile. A smile goes a long way toward putting yourself and the job interviewer at ease.

Ask a friend or relative to help role-play an interview by pretending to be your potential employer. When role-playing, have your friend sit behind a desk or table to make the practice interview realistic.

Give your "practice employer" a list of potential questions that may be asked. Whether in person or online, during your job interview, your task is to respond to each question as if you are on an actual job interview. Also, ask the "practice employer" questions, so you will feel more comfortable during the actual interview.

Practice on Zoom. If your interview will be online, practice and get familiar with how to use Zoom.

It's important to have a neatly typed *resume*. A resume includes your name, address, email address, telephone number, education, work history with dates, hobbies, civic work, social activities, and references.

For a professional-looking resume, research resumes online or check out books on resume writing from your library. Some job service agencies and colleges employ people who will help you write a resume for free. For a high-paying job, you may want to pay a professional to write your resume.

The reasons to have a neatly typed resume are:

Rich!

1.   A resume looks professional and shows you have a professional attitude toward work.

2.   You have a detailed description of necessary information when you are asked to fill out an application.

3.   Your resume can be quickly emailed if you telephone an employer and are told to first submit a resume.

Tips for the day of your interview whether online or in person:

- Allow yourself plenty of time to reach your interview destination.

- Arrive ten minutes early.

- Take a deep breath to get your nerves under control.

- Read over your practice notes and resume.

- Relax, smile, and do your best during the interview.

- As the interview wraps up, smile and thank the employer for the opportunity to interview.

Don't be discouraged if you don't get the job. Don't give up. Keep going on many interviews. And be happy when you do get the job!

If you discover a reference made a favorable impression with an employer, send that person a thank-you note. People appreciate being acknowledged for their efforts. They will remember your effort when they receive future calls from potential employers.

When you do get a job, don't go in with the attitude that it's the only job you'll ever have. Upward job mobility is the way of the future. Keep your eyes and ears open. There will be another job opportunity around the corner. Good performance at your present job will be a future job reference.

When considering your employment future, do what you enjoy and you can't go wrong! Sometimes the best jobs do not pay the most in the beginning. This is often the case in professions such as journalism, publishing, film, and television, to name only a few. A person usually must start at the bottom and work up. A job may be exciting and challenging, but it's a difficult choice if you're also faced with a job offer that pays more.

Think long and hard. I don't recommend giving up happiness for a few dollars more and a dull job that makes you unhappy. A lower-paying job with more chances now for creativity and higher pay in the future may be the route for you to follow.

In summary:

- **Tell everyone that you're searching for a job; that's networking!**

- **Design a world-class resume.**

- **Role-play for your job interview.**

- **Network with people in the profession you wish to pursue.**

- **Be prepared.**

- **You have one chance to make a first impression.**

- **Find a job that you enjoy!**

If you're not an 8 a.m. to 5 p.m. type person and you can't find a job you like, perhaps you need to create your own career. **Read on to *Chapter 15 – You're The Boss.***

CHAPTER 15
YOU'RE THE BOSS
Make It Work For You

More and more people are starting their own businesses. In *Chapter 2 – Setting Goals*, I suggested that shoveling snow on a snow day would be a good way to earn money; if you did this, you would create your own business. **You would be an entrepreneur, a person who organizes and manages a business!**

In the United States, a small business is defined as a business concern that is independently owned and operated, and is not dominant in its field of operation.

The **Small Business Administration (SBA.gov)** estimates that there are over 36 million small businesses in the United States.

Be aware that over 50% of small businesses dissolve within five years of opening. Dissolution includes business sales, mergers, acquisitions, and involuntary closures such as bankruptcies, failures, and terminations.

Don't let that stop you! The lack of proper research,

preparation, and working capital is what causes small business owners to fail.

What type of work do you want to pursue? Where do your talents lie?   Part-time and full-time businesses include graphic design, landscaping, carpentry, painting houses and fences, website development, walking and grooming pets, office filing and typing, computer repair, babysitting, accounting, house cleaning, research, auto mechanics, real estate, law, medicine, dentistry, or financial planning to name a few.   These jobs can be operated by an entrepreneur who is ***self-employed***.

Even if you plan to operate a part-time business, you should treat it as a profession from the beginning. Researching your tax responsibilities or consulting an accountant are first steps to starting your business. You'll need to know your tax responsibilities and advantages.

Self-employed people have tax deductions and tax privileges that aren't available to employed people. For instance, you can deduct costs of operating your business such as office rent, supplies, automobile expenses, tools needed in your business, office furniture, etc. Deducting the costs of operating your business means that the amount of taxes you pay are based on your net income rather than your gross income.

Many businesses can be operated from your home. According to the Small Business Administration, more than one-half of all U.S. businesses are based in an owner's home. The internet, electronic devices, computers, fax machines, and telecommunications systems make operating a business from home easier than ever.

The advantages of working from your home include:

- **Saving money on office rent. Tenant rent can be expensive for a new business on a tight budget.**

- **Saving time and money on transportation.** Not having to commute to and from an office saves time and money.

There can be drawbacks such as customers coming to your home and some businesses simply can't be operated from home. It takes a lot of discipline to work at home. A business owner can't be distracted, or let the work day be interrupted by poor work habits.

Conduct research and ask questions before sinking time or money into your own business. Read books on the subject, attend seminars, and talk to small business owners in your chosen profession.

Learn the answers to:

- **What do I like to do?**

- **Would people pay me for this service?**

- **What do business owners like and dislike about their profession?**

- **What education is required?** Some self-employed professions require college degrees, extensive education, or special licenses, certifications, or designations.

- **How did business owners get started?**

- **Ask business owners for suggestions and recommendations for being self-employed.**

- **What mistakes have business owners made in their businesses?**

- **What does it cost to get started?**

- **How do business owners advertise and market their businesses?**

- **What would business owners do differently?**

If starting your own business is intriguing, read lots of books and magazines for business owners. The Small Business Administration and local community colleges are good sources of information about owning and operating your own business.

By doing research, talking to business professionals, and reading books and magazines on your chosen profession, you'll decide whether you have what it takes to be a business owner.

In summary:

- **Business owners don't plan to fail, they may fail to plan.**

- **Obtain help for your business from organizations like libraries, community colleges, and the Small Business Administration.**

- **Treat your business as a profession from the start.**

- **Do what you love, and you'll love what you do!**

Whether you are a business owner or have a salary-paying job, one item that you will need at one time or another in your life is credit. Read on to the next chapter and learn how to get and keep

Rich!

good credit.

CHAPTER 16
CREDIT & CREDIT CARDS
A Word Of Caution

Good credit is a very good thing. By opening a checking account or savings account, you have established a form of credit.

To establish further credit, you can approach the banker where you have your checking or savings account and apply for a small loan … say, $100 to $500. The bank will require a completed application and proof of your ability to repay the loan. You may also be able to get a loan if a relative cosigns the loan (promises to pay if you don't).

You will establish good credit by making payments on time every month. A good payment history increases your chances of getting a larger loan in the future.

For many teenagers, as well as adults, your first major loan is for an automobile. You can finance a car through your bank, lending institution, or even the car dealership.

Many department and retail stores will extend credit to customers purchasing their products. However, interest rates on these consumer accounts can be very high and should be paid off entirely each month.

Seriously explore the world of borrowing money. You should know that negative consequences can result from being slow with payments or failing to repay the loan. Unfortunately, once a person gets into debt, getting out of debt can be difficult.

According to the Administrative Office of the U.S. Courts, there were 517,308 total bankruptcy filings in the United States during the 12-month period ending December 31, 2024. While this is a lower number of bankruptcies than in past years, this is still a significant number. Today, many Americans are seriously in debt. If handled improperly, credit cards can lead to serious financial problems.

Having good credit, and I emphasize *good* credit, is a very positive situation. **With good credit, a person can buy a car or a house with equal monthly payments.** This is a privilege because most people cannot afford to pay all cash for a car, much less a house. The misuse of credit can lead to financial disaster.

In *Chapter 6* we discussed how inflation compounding year after year can significantly increase your college costs. A similar situation develops with inappropriate borrowing. If people overspend with credit cards and do not pay off balances each month, they can find themselves in the position of paying out more than they earn. Many adults do not understand this concept. By making only minimum payments on credit cards, you can find it takes years to pay off the balance owed.

Credit card guidelines include:

1. **Avoid applying for multiple credit cards.** The lending institution where you bank can be a good source for one credit card.

2. **Compare credit card company interest rates and rewards**. Credit card interest rates typically range from 18% to 29%, with the average rate on existing balances at approximately 22.25%. However, credit card companies are competitive. They want your business. Therefore, do your research. By comparing, you will find a credit card company with a lower interest rate, and perhaps a better rewards program.

3. **Every time you make a credit card purchase, record the name and amount charged on a register such as a checkbook register.** Recording every credit card purchase and the amount that

you pay will help you keep track of all transactions and may help you limit the amounts you charge.

4. Charge only what you can pay off within one to three months. It's smart to pay off your credit card balance every month. Paying only the minimum monthly payment (approximately 2% of the balance) as many adults do, can lead to serious problems.

5. Be cautious if you receive unsolicited credit card offers in the mail. High-interest rates and annual fees may be attached to this card.

Credit card companies are in the business of making money. They may extend more credit than a person can handle.

Remember, "People don't plan to fail, they fail to plan." Treat borrowing money and credit cards like any investment venture. If your investments are paying 10% and your credit cards cost you 22.25% interest, you are losing money.

Here's a tip that you can share with your parents. If they have high interest on credit cards, suggest they call their credit card companies and negotiate lower interest rates. They can tell the credit card company that they are prepared to take their business (and the credit card company's way of making a living) to another credit card company with more competitive (lower) interest rates. Some credit card companies will lower interest rates and waive annual fees on the spot! Suggest your parents give it a try. It's worth a telephone call.

Be as cautious with your borrowing habits as you are with your savings and investments. Credit card debt has reached epidemic proportions in this country. Many people owe $30,000, $50,000, or more in credit card debt. Don't let yourself become part of that statistic. With high rates of interest, it could take 10 years or more to pay off credit cards if you only make the minimum monthly payment.

Avoid the credit-card merry-go-round:

- **Pay off credit card balances within one to three months. Preferably, pay your credit card balance off each month.**

- **Take an additional job, say part-time, to pay off credit cards as soon as possible.**

- **Negotiate the interest rates on credit cards.** For instance, if you have a credit card balance of $5,000 at 18% interest, you would pay approximately $900 a year in interest. If you can negotiate a new interest rate for 11%, the amount of interest paid would be lowered to $550 per year. That's a huge savings.

Lower interest rates on credit card debt can save a person hundreds to thousands of dollars every year. I suggest that any money saved by lower interest rates be used to pay the balance down on credit cards. That extra payment can help reduce the time it takes to pay off credit card debt.

In review, when dealing with credit and credit cards:

- **Establish good credit with a small loan and you will increase your ability to obtain larger loans to purchase a car, house, or business.**

- **Build good credit by making payments on time.**

- **Charge what you can pay off within one to three months.**

Enough on caution. Now consider your financial philosophy.

Read on to *Chapter 17 – Wrapping It Up.*

CHAPTER 17
WRAPPING IT UP
The Can-Do Philosophy

It's time to wrap it up! At this point you have received a lot of information about money management, financial planning, investments, financing post-secondary education, jobs, and credit.

Hopefully you know more about money management and finances now. However, if you think you know *all* there is to know about personal finances, you are incorrect.

Actually, your money management adventure is just beginning! As mentioned at the start, this book is a beginning when it comes to money management and the accumulation of wealth. What you have learned to this point is the basics. The basics are very helpful, although it's up to you to proceed further with your money management education. Commit to a "Can-Do Philosophy" and continue your financial education. You will find that there is a world of additional sources of information available to you.

There are publications that can give you useful and fun

information about investing. There are websites and magazines devoted to tips on saving, investing, and making money. The shelves of bookstores and libraries are full of books on how to invest in stocks, bonds, mutual funds, real estate ventures, getting into college, getting a job, starting a business, budgeting and financing your first car, a college education, or a home.

Your local library is virtually a gold mine of information … free of charge! Check out the **Reader's Guide to Periodical Literature** for recently published articles in periodical magazines and scholarly journals for helpful financial advice and information.

I encourage you to read the *Information Resources* section at the end of this book. Check out as many books as possible from your library and read them, physically or online. If you get only one idea from each book or article, you will be very, very rich in investment knowledge. Invest your time learning about finances and you will positively invest in your future! Develop your "Can-Do Philosophy".

There are also television programs devoted to the exploration of investments. A favorite of mine is Jim Cramer's *Mad Money*. Bloomberg and CNBC televise programs devoted to the subject of investments. Throughout the business day you will see stock market quotes across the bottom of the television screen and news-style programs with guest experts answering stock market and investment questions. Read biographies of well-known investors, such as Warren Buffett and Peter Lynch; it's enlightening to learn how they got to where they are by investing billions of dollars.

City and national newspapers have business sections which contain stock market topics and investment advice.

Get acquainted with a stockbroker, a mutual fund specialist, or financial planner. If you have a class project or paper to write, many business people will be happy to spend time answering your questions.

At first, in your quest for more knowledge about investments, the material you read or the television programs you watch may seem confusing. If you are patient and continue to read financial magazines and books, and watch financial television programs, eventually the investment lingo will make sense. That's when money management, finances, and investing become fun!

My wish is that you will continue your search for information about investments and the management of money. By being persistent and inquisitive, you shall reap the financial benefits. May you be rich in health, wealth, and wisdom! Best wishes and success!

GLOSSARY

A dictionary is a wonderful source of information. I recommend that you use one daily to learn the meaning of words. This glossary has been included to help you understand the advice and principles taught in this book.

annual fees – the yearly fees paid by the owner of a mutual fund to the mutual fund to cover expenses such as administration costs. Also, yearly fees charged by credit card companies.

annual report – a statement published yearly regarding a company's state of affairs.

annuities – investments yielding fixed payments during the annuity owner's life, for a certain number of years, or indefinitely.

asset allocation – the process of dividing your investment dollars among several different investment options to help reduce investment risk.

assets – the value of possessions owned by a person, including cash, savings, stocks, bonds, gold and silver bullion, real estate, and other investments.

balanced – the state of things being equal.

bankruptcy – the state of being legally declared unable to pay your debts, whereby your property is administered for the benefit of creditors and divided among them.

blue-chip – terminology used to explain large, well-known companies considered to be leaders in their industry.

board of directors – a group of individuals chosen to direct the affairs of a corporation or institution.

bondholder – a person who owns a bond issued by a company, government, or person.

bonds – interest-bearing certificates issued by companies or governments promising to pay a specific sum on a specific date.

bullion – gold or silver cast into a bar or other convenient shape.

cash value – the amount of money that is available to an insured for their own use, while keeping the insurance coverage in effect.

capital – wealth; money or assets used to produce more wealth.

certificates of deposit (CD) – a bank certificate acknowledging the receipt of a specified sum of money in a special kind of time deposit drawing interest and requiring written notice for withdrawal.

checkbook register – the written record of checks written and deposits made in a checking account.

claims – demands for insurance coverage by insureds when losses occur.

commodities – basic items or staple products traded, such as agricultural products.

common stock – an investment that represents ownership in a corporation. There is no definite dividend rate and it does not have the privileges of preferred stock, but usually gives an owner a vote at shareholders' meetings in proportion to shares owned.

common stock shareholders – the owners of common shares of a company's stock.

compounded – interest on the original interest amount plus the accumulated interest which accrues at regular intervals.

conventional bank mortgage – a mortgage obtained through a recognized banking institution with interest rates that are the going rate.

credit – money made available by a bank or other lending institution.

debits – entries or checks written in a checkbook register that decrease the amount of money in said checking account.

debt instrument – an investment that is evidence of debt issued by corporations and governments.

dependent – a student who relies upon parents or guardians for financial support.

disability – that which disables, as an illness or injury.

discount – the price at which a bond sells that is below its face amount.

disposable income – income that is available to spend after all taxes have been paid.

diversified – to vary or divide up investments among different companies, securities, types of investments, etc. A diversified investment portfolio can help reduce investment risk.

dividend – money paid to stockholders as income for investing in a company.

dollar-cost averaging – the practice of contributing a specified dollar amount to an investment on a regular basis, say monthly. In principle, the cost of buying an investment averages, so a person is not always buying at a high or low price per share.

Dow Jones Industrial Average – is a stock market index of 30 prominent companies listed on stock exchanges in the United States.

down payment – the amount of cash a buyer pays toward the total sale price of a home. Usually the dollar amount remaining (sale price minus down payment) will be covered by a home mortgage.

duplex house – a house consisting of two separate family units.

ending balance – the amount of money in your checking account as of the date of the bank's monthly statement.

entrepreneur – a person who organizes and manages a business undertaking, assuming the risk for the sake of the profit.

equity – the value of a property beyond the total amount owed on it in mortgages, liens, etc.

equity instrument – an investment that is evidenced by ownership in a corporation.

escrow – a written agreement, as a bond or deed, put in the care of a third party and not delivered or put in effect until certain conditions are fulfilled.

expenditures – expenses.

face amount – the amount of a bond on which interest is calculated.

financial advisor – a person who advises investors on financial matters.

fixer-upper – a house that needs improvements made, such as repairs and remodeling, to reach its full potential.

flavor of the month – a mutual fund that is favored by investors due to a large amount of publicity.

gross income – total income earned before taxes are taken out.

hypothetical/hypothetically – based on, involving, or having the nature of, a hypothesis; assumed; supposed.

implementing – to carry into effect; fulfill; accomplish.

independent – a college student who is not reliant upon parents or guardians for his/her source of income.

individual retirement account (IRA) – a type of retirement investment where the amount invested and accumulated interest are tax deferred.

inflation – an increase in the price of goods and services expressed as a percentage rate.

initial public offering (IPO) – shares of stock issued for people to purchase when a company needs to raise money.

institutional investors – investors such as large banks and insurance companies who invest very large sums of money and often are given preferential treatment regarding sales charges, etc.

insured – a person whose life, property, etc., is insured against loss.

investment portfolio – the investments of an individual or entity.

junk bonds – types of bonds generally considered to be inferior; below investment grade.

maturity – the time at which a bond, etc., becomes due.

mortgage – the pledging of property to a creditor as security for the payment of a debt.

mutual funds – a pooling of investors' money that is invested in various securities as determined by a trust or corporation's objectives.

Rich!

negotiate – decide, settle, or conclude (a personal or business transaction).

net – the amount of money remaining after taxes are paid.

net asset value (NAV) – the value of a mutual fund's shares calculated by subtracting expenses incurred by a mutual fund from the value of a mutual fund's assets, and then dividing that amount by the number of shares in the mutual fund.

net gain – income or profit remaining after expenses have been deducted.

net income – the amount of income remaining after all taxes are paid.

net loss – the amount of loss after all expenses are subtracted.

networking – exchanging ideas and information with a group of people or individuals.

New York Stock Exchange – the organization that regulates matters related to trading New York Stock Exchange listed securities and the conduct of its members.

novice – a person who is a beginner to an activity or occupation.

owner-financed – a real estate loan where the property owner accepts payments (and retains ownership of the property) from the buyer until the property is completely paid.

philosophy – theory or logical analysis of the principles underlying conduct, thought, knowledge, and the nature of the universe; included in philosophy are ethics, logic, metaphysics, etc.

preferred stock – stock on which dividends must be paid before those of common stock; it usually also receives preference in the distribution of assets.

premiums – systematic payments made to cover the cost of insurance. Premiums may be paid monthly, quarterly, semi-annually, or annually.

principal – the amount of a debt, investment, etc., minus the interest, or on which interest is computed; the face value of a stock or bond.

procrastinate – to put off doing something unpleasant or burdensome until a future time; to postpone.

prospectus – a written statement outlining the main features of a mutual fund. A prospectus may include investment strategy, expenses, fees, and management philosophy.

Reader's Guide To Periodical Literature – a reference tool, available through libraries, to recently published articles in periodical magazines and scholarly journals, organized by article subject.

reconcile – determine the amount in your checking account by adding and subtracting deposits and checks written as compared with the monthly written statement received from your bank.

research reports – a report of valuable information about the operation, credit worthiness, and management of a company.

resume – a document of a person's professional background, including career experience, skills, and education.

return – the amount of interest or income received on an investment.

self-employed – a person who owns their own business.

shareholders – owners of a company's stock.

Small Business Administration – an organization that assists owners of small businesses with the operation of their businesses.

socially responsible – a type of mutual fund that invests only in companies that are considered friendly to the environment and society in general.

Social Security taxes – taxes that are withheld from a person's income that help pay for disability and retirement benefits.

stock – an individual ownership in a company evidenced by a certificate.

stock brokerage – a company that acts as an agent in the buying and selling of stocks and bonds.

subsidized – financially supported by a third party, often from government sources, to a private enterprise, to help reduce costs to the public, such as a student.

supply and demand – an economic theory that the quantity of goods or services (supply) offered for sale at a given price is fueled by the desire to own or use (demand) that product or service.

tax bracket – the percentage of taxes a person pays based upon annual income less allowable deductions.

tax deferred – a type of investment where taxes are not paid until the investment is cashed in.

tenant – a person who pays rent to occupy or use a building or land.

term life insurance – a type of life insurance that does not accumulate cash value. Because term life insurance premiums only pay for the cost of insurance, premiums are usually low at a young age.

U.S. Treasury bills (also known as T-bills) – short-term debt securities of the U.S. government, sold in terms ranging from four weeks to 52 weeks, sold at a discount to its face value.

U.S. Treasury notes – medium-term debt securities with fixed interest payments, issued by the U.S. government and having maturities of two to ten years.

U.S. Treasury bonds – long-term debt securities with fixed interest payments, issued by the U.S. government and having maturities of twenty or thirty years.

unearned income – income that a person earns from sources such as stocks, bonds, mutual funds, and savings accounts.

whole life insurance – a type of life insurance that accumulates cash value that can be used by the insured. Whole life insurance premiums generally stay the same as the insured ages.

yin and yang – in Chinese philosophy, yin is the passive, negative, feminine force or principle in the universe contrasted with and complementary to yang, the active, positive, masculine force or principle in the universe. Chinese philosophy states that for the universe (and your life) to function properly, a balancing of yin and yang must be in effect.

INFORMATION RESOURCES

There are hundreds of personal finance, investment, money management, real estate books, newspapers, magazines, websites, and television programs that will super-charge your investment knowledge. Read, listen, and watch as many as you can.

Books

Buffett, Warren and Bevelin, Peter. *A Few Lessons for Investors and Managers from Warren Buffet.* PCA Publications, 2012.

Cramer, Jim. *How to Make Money in Any Market.* Simon & Schuster, 2025.

Hill, Napoleon. *Think and Grow Rich!* Original publication 1937.

Lynch, Peter. *Beating the Street.* Simon & Schuster, 2012.

Sorkin, Andrew Ross. *1929: Inside the Greatest Crash in Wall Street History – and How It Shattered a Nation.* Viking, 2025.

Financial Magazines & Publications (print & online)

Barron's
Bloomberg Businessweek
The Economist
Entrepreneur
Financial Analysts Journal
Forbes
Fortune
Inc.
Investment News
Investors Business Daily
Kiplinger's Personal Finance

MarketWatch
Money
Morningstar
Newsweek
Reuters
Time Magazine
U.S. News & World Report
The Wall Street Journal
Yahoo! Finance

Television News & Analysis

Bloomberg *Business News*
Bloomberg – *Wall Street Week*
Jim Cramer's Mad Money – CNBC
Fast Money – CNBC
PBS *NewsHour*
Power Lunch – CNBC
Squawk Box – CNBC
Squawk on the Street – CNBC

www.ingramcontent.com/pod-product-compliance
Lightning Source LLC
Chambersburg PA
CBHW060856170526
45158CB00001B/384